SUMMER EDITION

#HOME

101 Ways to Improve Your Home's Comfort & Energy Efficiency

SCOTT FISCHER

Ciel Publications

Table of Contents

Foreword

It has been six years since Ciel Power, LLC was started. In my case, it has been six full years with hundreds of residential energy retrofits and thousands of home energy audits. A lot has happened in the interim – with my family, my business, and my life. Many wonderful things, many good things, and many painful things. And, as this is written on the day of Muhammed Ali's passing, "It's not the strength of your skill but the power of your will that makes a champion." These words from Ali, along with the support of friends, family, and other inspirational figures like Ali, have helped carry me through both good and bad days to find myself sitting here writing this book.

In these six years, Ciel has accomplished perhaps more than any other company in its industry, and it has faced its share of challenges, perhaps equally as great. Ciel has created new markets and opportunities to expand energy efficiency through its municipal, community, and corporate partnerships; with these successes, we've had our challenges as we've worked to scale this business upwards and deliver our offerings to a greater volume of people. Along the way, we've put together an incredible group of individuals working together every day to make a difference in our state, our towns, and our neighborhoods.

To deliver our vision of cleaner, more responsible, and more efficient neighborhoods, we knew we needed to recruit the support and the backing of the homeowners, political establishments, business owners, and spiritual leaders in the communities in which we served. My partner Steve and I left a large corporate organization that had grown tremendously over the past thirty years using a business model that relied heavily upon the strength of its business relationships. Our intent was to bring a similar professional, ethical, and moral philosophy to a broader audience as we worked to grow the visibility of our small, bootstrapped energy efficiency company and therefore gain traction and awareness in a relatively obscure marketplace.

This vision of a "professional grade" process helped Steve and me spend endless hours designing websites, landing pages, brochures, fliers, home energy audit reports, business cards, posters, campaign logos, and marketing verbiage for our new business. We sought to dominate the industry almost immediately through sheer will and a relentless work ethic. With countless twenty-hour days and the help of some very talented individuals, we came out of the gate with top-flight reporting and marketing pieces reminiscent of our 'corporate' days, which had never been seen before in a field that had very few quality marketing initiatives.

We hit the market hard ahead of a cold winter, high energy prices, and generous incentives that combined to generate enough tailwind for us to open a small office and begin to hire employees. In our dogged pursuit of every resource that might help us take our fledgling business another step forward, we came across a "business accelerator" program that was designed to help new "green" businesses get off the ground. They provided a rich and abundant office environment in a professional office building at an affordable rate, allowing us to move from our living and dining rooms into this new setting, where we could give our employees a more structured and professional work environment.

Shortly after relocating into our new space, almost as if by accident, an email arrived about a small town in New Jersey seeking the services of a residential energy auditing firm to partner with their municipality to promote home energy audits and their related retrofits. The municipality had received a grant from the U.S. Department of Environmental Protection as part of a pilot program to develop "climate showcase" communities by developing and implementing a series of environmental action items that would help reduce the collective environmental footprint of municipal, corporate, and residential structures. As it turns out, the membership of their "green team" and the committee, tasked with these challenges, sought to create a meaningful reduction in the energy consumption of single family homes in their community, far beyond simply "handing out light bulbs at street fairs."

Their ideas were to build awareness within their community of a little-known energy efficiency incentive program that offered cash-back and financing incentives to homeowners taking a "whole-house" approach to reducing household energy consumption. The group sought to partner with a private, for-profit company, who would be motivated by entering into a joint partnership with the municipality. The group smartly hoped to combine their resources with those of a private entity that could bring additional marketing resources to their campaign and thus significantly increase participation levels through their combined efforts.

As a way to encourage homeowners to take the first steps towards participation, the township issued a Request for Proposal (RFP) seeking the services of a municipal home energy audit provider who would join their partnership and work with key members of their committee and green group to develop customized marketing campaigns and provide ongoing reporting as to the results of the combined effort.

With virtually no experience and for almost no reason beyond brute determination, a shared vision, and the marketing infrastructure we had built, we jumped headfirst into what would eventually become the first of many partnerships with municipalities, corporations, and non-profit organizations.

Because of our work together, the Highland Park program was one of the most successful programs that had ever been seen in the history of grassroots residential energy efficiency initiatives, with home energy audits performed on more than ten percent of the homes in this small New Jersey town. More than one hundred homes in the town were successfully retrofitted with air-sealing, insulation, and in some cases, new high-efficiency mechanical equipment.

Our success awakened other municipalities that had been struggling to gain traction with similar efforts in their own municipalities, and Ciel's presence began to grow. Ciel was selected to design, manage, and execute similar campaigns throughout the state of New Jersey. Sustainable Princeton selected Ciel to administer Princeton's town-wide energy efficiency program, supported in part by Princeton University.

Following Highland Park, Ciel entered into partnerships with municipalities across New Jersey, including Woodbridge, Millburn, Summit, Watchung, and Glen Rock. The success of these programs propelled Ciel's momentum in the energy efficiency space and helped Ciel become New Jersey's premier provider of home energy audits and energy efficiency upgrades, culminating with the 2016 Energy Star Century Club Award.

In short, the relentless grind has never let up, even after six years, thousands of home energy audits, and hundreds of retrofitted homes. Next week, the national Energy Star program will present their Century Club Award to our company in a presentation at the New Jersey Board of Public Utilities. This award is the culmination of six exhilarating, challenging, frustrating, exhausting, debilitating, boring, enlightening, and rewarding years spent forging a name for ourselves in the energy efficiency community.

Sustainability is a broad term that can be incorporated into a number of different contexts. Wikipedia defines sustainability as the "capacity to endure." Sustainability refers not only to our environment, but also to our cultures, economies, political systems, faiths, livelihoods, and existence as humans both in the context of our natural environment and in the context of our capacity as individuals to endure.

Our portfolio includes work performed for corporate sustainability leaders, principal shareholders of multi-national companies, preeminent historical societies, academic professors, and influential political leaders. The portfolio also includes installations for seniors, small business owners, teachers, librarians, and administrative assistants. We're very proud of the fact that the work we do spans all walks of life and touches homeowners from every economic, religious, ethnic, and cultural background.

This book, then, is the product of years of both academic and practical knowledge and, despite all of our ground-breaking successes, comes to you largely out of a personal failure. It has become evident to me that the business model associated with retrofitting the world's housing stock is not a scalable one as it exists today in America or, for that matter, anywhere else in the world. In recent years, many companies have advanced into the energy efficiency retrofit marketplace, only to turn around in a hasty retreat away from this important market. Reasons vary, but in business, it is important to be able to exercise a degree of control over the environment in which you conduct business. The variables associated with energy efficiency upgrades are almost innumerable, and as such, they don't lend themselves well to a large-scale enterprise.

The good news is that these variables do lend themselves very well to a one-on-one conversation, and many of the things that will help improve the sustainability of your environment are fairly easy to do. In this book and future books like it, I hope to convey the experiences I've had with many thousands of homeowners over the years, which have provided me with much of the knowledge that I hope to share with you.

In my years in business, many of my clients have asked me to share some of the most important things they can do to improve the sustainability of their homes so that they could better apply these things to their daily lives. This book answers many questions that homeowners have asked over the years, offering advice from simple behavior changes to entire mechanical upgrades that will help improve the comfort, energy efficiency, and sustainability of the homes we live in.

Introduction

If you own a home, or if you want to live a more sustainable lifestyle, this book was written for you.

It represents thousands of hours worth of work we have done in homes over the past years. It encompasses behavioral, technological, and practical ideas created and supported by the experiences we've had with thousands of homeowners with whom we've worked.

It is a belief that says the responsible consumption of energy is our obligation as citizens of this planet; a shared belief among many of the customers with whom we've worked. We've discovered most of the people we're interacting with have a mutual desire to lower the environmental impact of their household and they are willing to embrace the changes necessary to do so.

Indeed, the problem is not that the homeowners in this country don't want to make the changes necessary to reduce their environmental impact, the problem is that they haven't begun to understand where to start on the journey towards a more sustainable lifestyle.

As a result, we go on about our daily lives thinking our house is old and will always cost a fortune to cool during the summer months. We don't realize the enormous impact that small changes to our collective lifestyles can have on our natural environment.

Our environment is experiencing unprecedented changes with carbon dioxide levels higher than they've been at any time during the past 400,000 years, topping 400 parts per million. If fossil-fuel burning continues at this rate, these carbon dioxide levels will rise to upwards of 1,500 parts per million over the next few centuries which would take tens of thousands of years to reverse.

The effects of climate change is already being felt across the world. Average temperatures have begun to rise, ice is melting worldwide, sea levels are rising, and severe storms and droughts are occurring with more frequency and ferocity. The rest of the bad news is that, despite all of the media coverage and the worldwide agreements to lessen our global impact on the environment, very little change has begun.

Why is this? Why do we continue to destroy the environment in which we live? Why do we continue to consume and pollute with such reckless abandon? Why is it that with all the research available on climate change, we still find ourselves debating whether or not it exists?

This book does not answer those questions. This book is about giving you a bunch of simple ideas, that, if you read and absorb, will give you the power to make a difference in this big world in which we live.

Most of these ideas can be implemented for little or no cost. Many of these changes are small adjustments to daily habits that have become ingrained in us over many years of repetition. Others are more significant investments that can sometimes be made with the assistance of state and federal incentives.

So if our objective is to change – as it must be for our children and grandchildren to have a healthy, clean environment – we must change first. The first change that needs to take place has to do with your idea of what sustainability really is and what it takes to lead a more sustainable lifestyle. Once you've begun down this path, you'll meet lots of wonderful people along the way like I have, and I can assure you that your life and your relationships will take on new vitality and new meaning. You'll see a more meaningful and rewarding life unfold before you and this vitality will make its way into other aspects of your life, like the food you eat, the amount of exercise you get, and the way you feel about yourself.

I've seen it happen hundreds of times, in every socioeconomic level, with people who knew nothing about sustainability when they started. My wish is that by the time you are through reading this book, you will have joined the millions of people around the world who are working to make our environment a cleaner and healthier place.

Window Treatments

Most work in the energy efficiency space outside of appliances, lighting, and mechanical equipment is done in the attic, basement, and wall-cavities of the homes in which we work. There are normally very few opportunities for us "energy efficiency types" to delve into the colors, patterns, shapes, and designs that add to the home's aesthetic, with one exception: window treatments.

Drapes and curtains work to reduce summer heat transfer in two ways. An insulating window covering slows the transfer of heat into the home, reducing the need for a home's cooling system to combat latent heat gain. Light-colored backing works to reflect the heat of the sun outward, rather than inward to be quickly absorbed by furnishings or other items.

A material's resistance to temperature is measured using a term called R-Value, and the right combination of window treatments can effectively double the insulating value of a typical premium window. If your windows are older single-pane windows, the addition of the right combination of window treatments will likely have an even larger impact on the comfort and energy efficiency of a room.

Double-pleated honeycomb shades can be a good option for folks who prefer to keep it simple. In a recent interview for *House Logic*, Ann Werner, sales team supervisor for Blinds.com, says a double-pleated honeycomb shade prevents energy loss as efficiently as a 1/8-inch sheet of rigid foam insulation and that most double-pleated honeycomb shades have R-values between R-2 to R-5.[1]

When fully closed, the R-value of thermally lined drapes can top that of double-pleated honeycomb shades, coming in between R-3 and R-5 depending on the type of fabric and the thickness of the lining and interlining. This efficiency, coupled with the infinite variety of colors, styles, and patterns, makes draperies one of our favorite ways to improve the comfort and efficiency of a space while adding character and style to a room.

Most of us prefer not to live with all of our draperies and blinds closed, particularly during spring and summer months, so another option is to utilize a product that will diffuse indoor sunlight to reduce heat gain. This can be accomplished using a variety of different window treatments, including sheer curtains and translucent honeycomb shades, that will help dilute the sun's rays when installed, but simultaneously allow the sunlight to brighten the room.

Blinds & Curtains

According to Hunter Douglas, "Windows without coverings are like valves that are always open." When we add window coverings to bare windows, we are adding "valves" - but unlike most valves that control the flow of liquid or gas, window coverings control the flow of energy.[2]

During summer months, both solar and heat energy flow from outside the home through the windows and into the living space. This increases the load on the home's cooling system as well as comfort-related issues. Close curtains and blinds when direct sunlight shines on the window. Leave curtains and blinds closed if you will not be home during daylight hours.

According to the U.S. Department of Energy, reflective blinds that are completely closed and lowered on a sunny window can reduce heat gain by around 45%, with the added benefit of having the ability to reflect the light onto a brightly colored ceiling that can diffuse the light throughout the room without much heat or glare.[3]

The ability of draperies to reduce heat loss and gain depends on several factors. Although difficult to generalize because of the wide variety of fabric types and colors, a medium colored drapery with white backings can reduce indoor heat gain by one third.

Solar Films

Single-Pane, unshaded windows transmit about 85% of the solar heat striking them. This can account for up to 40% of a home's accumulated heat.[4]

To keep natural light flowing through your home or to treat windows lacking curtains or blinds, consider adding window film to the surface of the window glass. If your windows were manufactured without low-e coating (closely check the pane of the glass for a low-e marking, or hold a white piece of paper near the outside of the window and if the reflection is not white, they are likely low-e), window film will allow light to enter the home while blocking much of the heat and UV rays.

According to window film manufacturer 3M, their Sun Control Window Films "reject up to sixty percent of the heat coming through your windows," while allowing up to "seventy percent of the visible light through your windows."[5]

The U.S. Department of Energy says that the silver, mirror-like films are typically more effective than the colored, more transparent ones, and that east and west facing windows will benefit most because of their greater potential for heat gain. North facing windows won't benefit from them and south-facing windows may benefit somewhat, but that benefit could be offset by the reduction of heat transfer from the winter sun during heating seasons. Window films are best used in climates with long cooling seasons, because they also block the sun's heat in the winter.

High Efficiency Windows

Depending on your climate, window manufacturers provide a wide array of products, offering higher levels of light filtering for southern climates, while offering balanced products for seasonal climates experiencing both heating and cooling seasons.

Window options include coatings, gasses, and multiple panes of glass encased within the same window to offer varying levels of energy efficiency depending on your budget and the climate in which you live. RESNET, the Residential Energy Services Network, recommends replacing old windows with "quality windows that will last a long time," suggesting that "you will realize great savings over time through increased energy savings."[6] They recommend that individuals in the market for replacement windows brush up on energy rating labels, which allow consumers to quickly compare the efficiency of products from various manufacturers.

The features of an ideal replacement window vary by climate. RESNET recommends becoming familiar with window energy ratings, choosing the proper glass, purchasing from a reputable manufacturer, and hiring a qualified installer.

Lighting

LED lighting uses only twenty to twenty-five percent of the energy of traditional incandescent bulbs, and bulbs last up to twenty-five times as long.[7] An efficient and sustainable option, these bulbs come in a variety of colors, brightness levels, and shapes, and they fit in almost any fixture.

According to weekly environmental news and information program "Living on Earth," LEDs are more closely related to computer technology than they are to traditional incandescent lighting.[8] LED, or light-emitting diode, bulbs are essentially two semi-conductors that, when energized, allow electrons to jump from one material to the other. As the electrons jump, they emit energy in the form of photons, and the color of light created by a given LED depends on the amount of energy in the photon. This, in turn, depends on the material used for the layers.

ElectronicsWeekly.com says, "General lighting LED applications continue to gain traction in both commercial and residential markets."[9] General lighting applications account for around 57% of the almost twenty-six billion dollar LED market projected for 2018, with the remainder allocated to signage, automotive lighting, mobile devices, displays, and monitors.

In the very near future, lighting options will no longer be limited to sockets and fixtures, as newer technology allows lighting to become fully integrated into a wide variety of building products, including panels, tiles, wallpaper, and conventional household items. At this year's 2016 LED Symposium and Expo, lighting manufacturer LG introduced the next generation of lighting: flexible OLED (Organic Light-Emitting Diode) lighting.[10] Featuring light-emitting panels made from organic materials that emit light when electricity is applied, these panels are the closest to natural light since the incandescent bulb, and their flexible shapes and sizes will allow an endless array of applications.

In the near future, LED lighting will add new colors, style, and flair to our homes, automobiles, shopping centers, and venues. Already emerging at concerts, fashion shows, sporting events, and retail outlets, the creative uses of LED and the emerging OLED technologies know virtually no bounds and are poised to dramatically change the way we think of light being delivered to the spaces we occupy.[11]

Tech Tip: Newer bulbs include color, brightness, timing, and even musical options that can be controlled remotely from your smart phone.

Green Roofs

Although not for everyone, green roofs are ideal for urban buildings with flat or shallow-pit roofs. In addition to keeping the space beneath cooler, green roofs also help mitigate rainwater runoff, provide sunny space for gardens, produce oxygen and nourishment for occupants, and provide a pleasant environmental aesthetic while reducing seasonal cooling loads.

In a Forbes Magazine article entitled "6 Busted Green-Roof Myths," author and architect Mariana Pickering debunked many of the common myths surrounding green roofs, including the most common myths that "green roofs are only for ecobuffs, they're high maintenance and they're experimental and risky," adding that they are "all untrue."[12]

Green roofs have been around for centuries, but the thinner and lighter roof profiles of late have brought about a resurgence of this unique building option. Examples of green roofs constructed in the 1940s are still scattered throughout Germany and Norway, where green-roofed houses are still "quite sought after."

Perhaps the most common concern associated with green roofs is that they might be more prone or susceptible to leaking. Mariana suggests that roofs are leaky, "independent of whether it's a green roof or a traditional roof," and recommends that all roofs have a proper waterproofing membrane, green roofs included. She says, " A properly designed green roof will also have a root barrier to stop plants from trying to root too deep," and cites studies suggesting that green roofs may have a longer life due to the waterproof membrane's protection from ultraviolet light.

The designed loads of green roofs can be accounted for in a newly constructed home, but retrofit green roofs require a careful assessment of the structure and proper planning of materials, plants, and drainage systems. Consult a professional before installing to ensure the suitability of your roof. Visit greenroofs.org for additional information.

Shading

Research has shown that temperatures can be 3 to 5 degrees cooler in tree-shaded neighborhoods than in treeless areas. Beyond adding to your home's curb appeal, well-placed plants, trees, shrubs, and foundation plantings deliver shade and act as windbreakers to buffer extreme wind and temperatures. A carefully thought out landscape can lower summer energy consumption anywhere from fifteen to fifty percent. One Pennsylvania study reported air-conditioning savings as high as seventy-five percent in small mobile homes.[13]

To conserve energy for summer shade, the Arbor Day Foundation recommends planting trees on the west and northwest sides of the home to provide mid-to-late afternoon shade in most locations.[14] The Foundation also suggests planting shade trees over patios, driveways, and air-conditioning units and keeping lower branches pruned to prevent obstruction of the views offered by these windows.

The website Earth Times suggests opting for deciduous trees in climates with cold winters, which will allow the sun's rays to reach the house once the tree has shed its leaves ahead of winter. This allows the home to be warmed by the sun's rays during the colder winter months and lessens the burden on the home's heating system.[15]

Tip: The proper placement of only three trees will save an average household between $100 and $250 in energy costs annually.

Tip: For additional sustainability benefits, consider a plant's water consumption, pesticide requirement, future growth, and fertilizer needs before adding to your home's landscaping. Many plants, particularly those native to your environment, may offer the additional benefits of lower water, and pesticide requirements.

Lattice, Trellises, or Window Boxes

A lattice, trellis, or window box can help diffuse direct sunlight. Strategically placed along the home's perimeter or facade, these items can improve a home's visual appeal while also providing shade and admitting cooling breezes to the area.

Jennifer Stimpson of *This Old House Magazine* says, "A wall covered with climbing vines may benefit the fairy-tale suitor who scales it to reach his true love, but in the real world the twisting tendrils will wreak havoc on your house's siding. Better that you create a buffer between the foliage and the facade with a garden trellis." Stimpson continues, "Not only will it provide the plants with a more appropriate host, but it will also give you something better than a blank wall to look at when summer's greenery fades."[16]

Available in wood, metal, plastic, string, and bamboo, trellises can be paired with fences or screens, attached directly to homes, or left freestanding supported by posts in the ground. A trellis fence or screen can be as simple as a few stakes in the ground or as complicated as systems of interlocking pillars.

Kilian Ganly of All Decked Out, a New York City landscape design-build firm, suggests in an article for SC Johnson's *Right at Home* to "match your garden style. Formal gardens with rectilinear lines and sharp corners look best with streamlined wood-lath and lumber trellises. For rustic or cottage gardens, invest in quirky free-form materials and vintage accessories." Ganly continues, "Gingerbread lattices with Victorian trim enhance romantic gardens."[17]

Ganly also recommends considering your garden's scale when selecting a trellis. "A large architectural arch might overwhelm an intimate backyard space…Think of repurposing household items including wooden ladders, fence posts, lattice, and lathe into a decorative trellis." For those of us who are less crafty, Ganly suggests investigating prefabricated trellises available through garden retailers and mail-order catalogs.

Whatever your method, a strategically placed trellis can add beauty and creativity to the landscaping of your home while helping to diffuse the sun's rays.

Programmable or Learning Thermostats

When Lindsey Turrentine, a journalist charged with reviewing the Nest learning thermostat for CNET, chose to purchase her Nest unit rather than return it to the company, she noted, "When a tech journalist pays $250 for a thermostat, you know it's a special kind of thermostat."[18]

As a Nest Concierge Provider, we've had our share of hands-on experiences with this device, and we concur. The simplest programmable thermostats work on a timer, allowing you to program the unit to adjust the indoor temperature during away hours and adjust itself to a more comfortable setting ahead of your predetermined arrival time. Advanced learning thermostats work to intuitively understand your home's occupancy and preferred temperature and adjust these settings automatically.

Aesthetically pleasing and controllable via a smart phone, the Nest device updates itself automatically, continuously refining its capabilities and adding additional features with each new update. Turrentine says the savings generated in her home, which is located in the Bay Area and has heating but no air-conditioning system, totaled 15 percent, which equated to $70 for their 2,000 square foot home.

Acquired by Google in 2014, Nest Labs has also continued its roll-out of the "Works With Nest" platform, which allows other electronic devices to communicate with the Nest Learning Thermostat.[19] These connected devices range from light bulbs that turn themselves off and on based upon your occupancy to door locks that will unlock themselves and water heaters that lower their temperature while you are away. The thermostat is becoming ground zero for the emergence of the "internet of things."

Fans

The simple addition of a floor or table fan to your living space can save a significant amount of energy by improving comfort when a home's air-conditioning system is in use. Fans help us feel more comfortable by adding four to eight degrees of perceived comfort simply by circulating the air around us.

Prefer to be without air-conditioning? Jean Nick of Rodale's *Organic Life* uses his experience growing up in an old farmhouse with no air conditioning as a backdrop for his advice about strategic open windows and fan placement in his article, "How To Keep Your House Cool Without AC."[20]

According to Nick, the occupants of the home should only open windows when it is cooler outside than inside. In this instance, Nick suggests taking the additional step of creating a natural draft by "opening downstairs windows on the shady side of the house and upstairs windows on the hot side of the house." Nick suggests increasing this natural air-flow by putting a portable window-mounted fan in the upstairs window.

Nick suggests experimenting with how wide you open the windows, as "it only takes a few inches downstairs." Nick suggests, "If you are leaving for the day, you will want to shut everything up before you go out."

On a side note, since beginning my research for this book, I've been loosely experimenting with this method and I've come to really appreciate the advice shared by Nick. At night, I find sleeping in the direct path of a fan uncomfortable, and a rotating fan with its periodic sweep back and forth is an irritant at best. I've been experimenting with Nick's suggestion of inserting a fan pointed outward in my upstairs bedroom window. The result has been a gentle breeze brought by air drawn up from the cooler lower levels of our home, and I've really come to enjoy it.

Duct Sealing

If you have a flat attic and there's something that looks like a big shiny octopus up there with tentacles running all over the place, it's likely the means of distribution for your home's heating and/or cooling system. And if it's summer, you've probably noticed that it's really hot up there.

A central air-conditioning system works by pulling air from the living space through a network of ducts called a return, conditioning the air, and then returning the conditioned air back to the living space via the supply ducts. Any leaks in this system can significantly reduce the efficiency and performance of the system.

By closely examining the supply and return network of ducts in your home and sealing up joints and connections with mastic, drawbands, and tape, you will be able to increase the performance and energy efficiency of your air-conditioning system.

According to Martin Holladay, author of Green Building Advisor's "Musings of An Energy Nerd," the joints of rigid ducts should be sealed with Mastic, "a gooey, non-hardening material with a consistency between mayonnaise and smooth peanut butter."[21] Sealing ducts is messy work, Halladay says, so he suggests wearing old clothes and using a disposable paintbrush or your fingers (with gloves on) to seal any gaps less than 1/8" thick. For gaps over 1/8", Holladay recommends first applying fiberglass mesh tape to the joint, then applying mastic onto the mesh tape to provide additional reinforcement. Mastic should be applied to the depth of "about a nickel."
Prioritize ducts running through a garage, as they are especially important. Return ducts are "pulling" air from your living space, which means that any gaps in the ductwork will result in noxious air from your automobiles getting pulled into the duct system and distributed by your home's air-handler throughout your home.

Duct Insulation

The U.S. Department of Energy says, "Ducts that leak heated air into unheated spaces can add hundreds of dollars a year to your heating and cooling bills." It also suggests that "insulating ducts in unconditioned spaces is usually very cost-effective."[22]

If you've noticed a foil "jacket" or a shiny "bubblewrap" over your ductwork, you're in good shape. But if the ductwork running through your garage or attic is uninsulated, simply adding R-8 insulation to these exposed ducts will improve your comfort and save money.

When insulating HVAC ductwork, use a foil faced insulation with an R-value of eight or higher. Seal connections with mastic and allow them to dry before applying duct insulation. Measure out manageable sections of insulation and cut to width and length using a square and sharp utility knife. Use metallic foil duct tape to seal and hold the insulation in place. Where sections of insulation come together, be sure to seal the underside of the joint by sliding the tape underneath the joint, then gradually removing the paper backing.

Air-Conditioning Systems

Like with most appliances, there's a variety of air-conditioning systems on the market with varying levels of energy efficiency. The energy efficiency of an air-conditioning system is rated using a "SEER" (Seasonal Energy Efficiency Ratio) Rating.

Units with higher ratings operate more efficiently through a combination of both practical and technological design. New air-conditioning systems are 20 to 40 percent more efficient than minimum-efficiency models made just ten years ago.

A common mistake often made when buying a new air-conditioning system is to purchase an "oversized" unit in an effort to deliver extreme cooling capabilities. To cool the air in your home, an air-conditioner extracts both heat and humidity. Oversized air-conditioning systems cycle on to bring down the temperature of the room quickly, but cycle off before the humidity has been removed from the air. This results in an uncomfortable "clammy" feeling, an increased likelihood of mold, and a strong likelihood of long-term damage to the system.

The consumer protection magazine *Consumer Reports* recommends having your contractor perform a "Manual J" load calculation on the home, which will take into account your home's size, orientation, insulation levels, window type, and other factors to recommend the proper-sized air-conditioning system for your home.[23]

Consumer Reports also recommends doing proper due diligence on your contractor, including checking their certifications, license, recommendations, and insurance information. The magazine says, "Be leery of a contractor who bases estimates merely on house size or vague rules of thumb."

Tip: Investigate mini-split systems for retrofit applications.

Ceiling Fans

Stationary and ceiling fans use significantly less energy than either window or central air-conditioning systems. Ceiling fans can work either separately or together with your air-conditioning system to deliver improved comfort and energy efficiency.

When air circulates, our body perceives the ambient temperature of the surrounding air to be four to eight degrees cooler than that of stationary air. On mild days, strategically placed ceiling fans may replace the need for air-conditioning, and when the air-conditioning system is being utilized, the additional air circulation will improve the comfort of your indoor space and likely allow the system to run at a higher temperature and reduce its consumption of energy.

Tip: Whole House Fans need to be used with caution, as these fans are sometimes powerful enough to reverse the flow of air from the atmospherically vented mechanical equipment in a home. As a result of this strong pull, exhaust air is pulled through the living space of the home rather than up the chimney as designed.

Filters

Perhaps the simplest and most effective way to improve the performance of your system, filter replacement is important to the overall effectiveness and energy efficiency of your air-conditioning system. We know you've heard this one before, but sometimes the filter goes unchanged despite our best intentions.

According to the U.S. Department of Energy, replacing a dirty filter with a clean one can lower your air conditioner's energy consumption by five to ten percent. When asked how often a filter should be changed, a recent blog post by O'Brien Service on the home improvement service website Angie's List said that "it depends."[24]

The post suggests that several factors need to be considered, "but the main rule of thumb is if it looks dirty, change it."[24] Other factors include the quality of the filter, the thickness, and other variations. O'Brien Service says to check the label to see what the manufacturer recommends and suggests that lesser quality filters will likely need to be replaced more frequently.[24]

Other consideration factors include whether or not anyone in the home suffers from allergies. If so, O'Brien suggests more frequent filter changes to remove more of the allergens from the air in your home.[24] Another thing to consider is how many dogs and cats live in the home, and the propensity of these animals to shed. Pet hair gets everywhere, including into your home's air-conditioning system.

Finally, in the thousands of homes we've checked out, we've noticed improperly sized filters, filter chambers that are missing a sealed door, and filter doors that were not securely closed after a replacement filter had been installed. All of these imperfections allow contaminants to bypass the filter and increase the likelihood of additional contaminants entering the air stream to pollute the indoor air and contaminate the duct system. To avoid this, make sure your system's filter chamber is sealed and the door is fully latched.

Supply and Return Ducts

Being sensitive to the location of your home's supply and return ducts when rearranging furnishings and installing wall hangings will allow your system to continue operating at its full capacity. Often, if nothing is felt coming through the register, homeowners feel comfortable blocking the register with furniture and wall hangings, not realizing that they are inhibiting the flow of return air through their system.

If your duct system includes flex duct, try gently pulling these runs taught to help smooth the interior surfaces of the duct which will help improve air-flow through the system. Elbows and ninety degree turns can also have a significant impact on the performance of your duct system. Keep interior surfaces smooth, turns gradual, and joints sealed to maximize your system's performance.

If you've tried these options and continue to have poor distribution of conditioned air, contact a Building Performance Institute Accredited Provider to schedule a "duct-blaster" test. During a duct-blaster test, technicians will pressurize your duct system to determine the overall leakiness of the system and inspect for catastrophic failures.

To properly size duct systems, request a Manual D calculation from your HVAC contractor. A Manual D is created using sophisticated software that incorporates information about your home and its mechanical equipment to create design calculations for use in servicing or installing your home's duct system.

Another common issue with a poorly performing air-conditioning system is an improperly sized return duct. Often, return duct(s) are too small to allow enough air to flow through the system. Increasing the size of the return duct or adding a return duct in another location can often lead to improved system performance.

Attic Insulation

One of the most effective ways to buffer extreme temperatures is to install the proper amount of insulation for your climate. In colder climates, recommended attic insulation levels can reach as high as R-60, or approximately 18" of cellulose or fiberglass insulation. Most homes were built before modern energy efficiency building codes. As a result, the amount of attic insulation is inadequate to buffer the extreme combination of radiant, conductive, and convective heat occurring during the summer months.

To understand insulation levels, it is important to understand how heat is transferred. According to Quinn Korzeniecki of the Building Performance Institute (BPI), heat transfer occurs in three ways: conduction, convection, and radiation.[25]

BPI suggests thinking of your morning coffee to better understand conduction. "Steaming hot liquid is placed in a paper cup, which you then hold in your hand. Without that extra cardboard sleeve, your hand will start to feel the heat pretty quickly. That is conduction: the transfer of heat between objects that are in contact."

According to Dictionary.com, convection is defined as "the transfer of heat by the circulation or movement of the heated parts of a liquid or gas." Korzeniecki suggests thinking of air traveling through a forced-air heating system. Heat, transferred from a burner to a heat exchanger to the air molecules moving through your furnace, is being pushed through your home's duct system to warm different parts of your home. The process of transferring heat using the circulation of warm air is convection.

Finally, Korzeniecki defines radiation as the "transfer of heat from a warm object through space to a cooler object. The objects do not have to be touching for successful heat transfer."

Korzeniecki adds that "Radiant heat transfer is generally the culprit for discomfort in a home."

Korzeniecki describes how summer heat travels through a home that has a conventional attic, saying, "On a hot day the sun's heat radiates onto the roof. The heat conducts through the roof assembly and radiates from the roof to the attic floor. The heat conducts from the attic floor to the ceiling below. The heat radiates to cooler surfaces in your living space."

R-value refers to a material's (r)esistance to heat flow. So, the greater the R-value of the insulation in your attic, the greater your attic's resistance to transferring heat radiating from above into the living spaces beneath the attic floor.

The process described by Korzeniecki is the reason many homeowners struggle to remain comfortable in the upper levels of their home during summer months. Homes with little or no insulation will often experience comfort issues in the upper regions of the home. Homeowners with upgraded attic insulation typically notice a significant improvement in the comfort levels of the upper regions of their homes.

Exterior Wall Insulation

According to the 2009 Residential Energy Consumption Survey, which used methods developed by the Lawrence Berkeley National Laboratory to estimate insulation levels, 90% of existing American homes are under-insulated.[26]

According to RESNET, the Residential Energy Services Network, most homeowners think of windows and doors when addressing home comfort issues because they are the most visible indicators of home energy efficiency problems. RESNET says, "What they don't realize is that insulation has a much greater impact (up to three times as much) on the average home's energy and comfort than windows or doors. Assessing a home's insulation takes only a few minutes, and the resulting improvements can produce a significant increase to home comfort, as well as substantial reductions to home energy bills."[27]

Exterior walls account for the greatest exposed surface area of most homes. As a result, improvements to the exterior insulation of your home can have a dramatic impact on a home's comfort and energy efficiency. In an existing home, consider using blown-in insulation, which, when properly installed using a dense pack technique, will offer the additional benefit of restricting air movement in the wall cavity in addition to its value as an insulation material.

Depending on your siding type, blown-in cellulose insulation can generally be added to wall cavities from underneath the existing siding on the exterior of the home. There's a higher level of difficulty associated with the proper installation of insulation, and it is typically not a do-it-yourself type project.

Basement Insulation

In colder climates, adding insulation to exposed basement walls, particularly those within three feet of ground level, is almost always cost-effective, and depending upon the type of insulation, it will lower the humidity level of the basement by helping to prevent moisture from entering the living space. A properly insulated basement will stay dryer and smell better than an un-insulated basement.

Martin Holladay of Green Building Advisor's "Musings of an Energy Nerd" suggests using closed-cell spray foam or polyisocyanurate rigid board foam to insulate basement walls. Halladay suggests avoiding fiberglass insulation in basements because of the likelihood of moisture in the interior air condensing against the cold surface of the concrete.[28]

For homeowners concerned about "locking" the moisture inside of the concrete or stone foundation, Holladay says, "...you don't want to encourage any moisture to enter your home. Your concrete wall can stay damp for a century; that dampness won't hurt the concrete."

Halladay suggests that homeowners inspect and repair any sources of moisture and review the applicable building codes regarding the installation of either rigid or spray foam insulation before insulating a basement. Many code requirements mandate that the insulation be protected by a layer of drywall to act as a buffer against possible sources of ignition.

Air-Sealing

Single handedly the most important and effective means of improving comfort and energy efficiency, air-sealing is a cost-effective way to improve comfort, reduce summertime energy bills, and keep insects, moisture, allergens, critters, and outdoor air outside.

Tom Harrison, Jr. of Energy Circle, LLC described on his blog how an energy audit, caulk, and insulation are saving him more than $1,000 per year. Harrison says, "My air sealing work and the benefits it reaped confirmed my long-held belief that air sealing should be step one in improving a home's energy efficiency...It's cheaper and easier than an insulation upgrade, and helps to ensure that insulation will remain effective."[29]

In his blog, Harrison highlights the infra-red pictures taken both before and after he performed the air-sealing measures on his home. The images were taken with the aid of a blower door, a device designed to simulate a twenty mile-per-hour wind, and they clearly show a dramatic difference in the air-leakage of his home. The blower door confirmed this reduction, measuring nearly a 50% reduction in air-flow through the home.

Air-sealing penetrations in the floor of your attic and along the above-grade portions of the exterior walls of your basement will provide the biggest "bang for your buck." Once these areas have been addressed, caulk around windows, doors, and floor moldings as needed to block air infiltration. If you're not sure about the air infiltration points in your home, schedule a home energy audit with a provider who uses a blower door. This device will depressurize your home and clearly identify air-sealing opportunities.

Of particular note, recessed lights in older homes are the functional equivalent of chimneys. If your home has older recessed lighting, particularly in ceilings connected to unconditioned space, an LED retrofit kit will likely not only lower your lighting cost, but also help reduce your heating and cooling costs by performing the additional task of sealing off your home's upper levels from the attic space above. This helps contain conditioned air within the living space rather than letting it escape through the attic.

Harrison says they are "much more comfortable in the home," but notes they've also come to realize that, "there's no silver bullet: improving the energy efficiency of our house is an ongoing process – there is still much to be done."

Crawlspace Encapsulation

Crawlspaces are common in many of today's homes, particularly those with additions. These areas are generally beneath living spaces and often contribute to comfort and moisture issues within the home.

Ventilated crawlspaces should be completely separated from the adjoining basement and the ceilings of these areas should be insulated from the living space above. One of the best materials to utilize for this application is spray foam insulation, which acts as an insulation material and an air-sealing material and is impervious to air and moisture.

Crawlspaces without ventilation should be connected to the adjoining basement to improve ventilation of the space. Dirt floors should be covered with a vapor barrier, and the walls of the crawlspace should be insulated using rigid foam boards or spray foam insulation.

Rim-Joist Insulation

The area of your home that meets its foundation is commonly referred to as the "rim joist." This area is the skinniest section of most houses, and it is the part most vulnerable to extreme temperatures. Additionally, it is common to discover a gap between these two sections of the home that may develop from settling, uneven blocks, and imperfections in the building materials.

Having a professional apply spray foam insulation to this section of the home will add an additional buffer from outdoor temperatures while also performing the added task of air-sealing to prevent outdoor air, insects, and moisture from entering the living space.

Smart Power Strips

Today's electronics use a significant amount of energy, in many cases while the appliance itself is not being utilized. One way to mitigate this energy consumption is to control the flow of energy to the device using a "smart" power strip. Smart power strips automatically cut off power to ancillary devices when they sense that a primary device has been turned off.

There are a number of variations of this product available on the market. Some variations utilize a remote control or wireless application to allow for additional control over the devices plugged into the power strip. Some variations of this device also allow for wireless monitoring of the amount of electricity being consumed by each device.

Smart power strips can be an effective tool to manage energy consumption in today's tech-heavy households.

Energy Star Rated Products

Perhaps the simplest and easiest way to reduce energy consumption is to purchase Energy Star rated appliances when replacing or upgrading existing appliances.

Administered by the United States Environmental Protection Agency and the United States Department of Energy, the ENERGY STAR program is the most successful voluntary energy conservation movement in history. Started in 1992, over three hundred and fifty billion dollars in savings has been attributed to the ENERGY STAR program. More importantly, the program has reduced greenhouse gasses by over two and a half billion tons since its inception.[30]

As a third party certification, experts test and analyze the quality, performance, and efficiency of products in more than seventy product categories. Additionally, the program certifies homes and commercial buildings with the ENERGY STAR label.

Tip: ENERGY STAR rated washing machines use 35% less water and 20% less energy than standard washers.

Fact: ENERGY STAR does not label clothes dryers because most of them use similar amounts of energy.

Cold Water Wash

In 2011, the non-profit organization Alliance to Save Energy, an organization devoted to the worldwide advancement of energy efficiency policies, products, and investment, partnered up with Proctor & Gamble to get the word out about cold water washing.[31]

According to the *New York Times*, after evaluating its energy footprint in 2003 and realizing how much energy was used for laundry, Proctor & Gamble set a goal to convert seventy percent of all washing-machine loads to cold water by 2020.[32] As of the publication of this book, an update on P&G's website says they have increased the global percentage of cold water loads from thirty-eight to fifty-three percent.[33]

In general, consumers worldwide have been slow to move toward cold water washing, with many concerned that washing in cold water alone will not clean clothes as well. According to James Danzinger, a senior scientist who works on detergents at Proctor and Gamble, thermal energy is one of the three secrets to cleaning clothes, along with mechanical energy and chemicals. In a *New York Times* article, Danzinger says, "When you reduce one, you have to do better in the others."

A little over ten years ago, Proctor & Gamble introduced Tide Coldwater, and several competing brands followed with competing cold-water formulas. With many brands of detergent containing completely different chemical compositions than their warm-water counterparts, these detergents are specifically meant for cold-water washing.

Consumer Reports Magazine had high marks for Tide's Coldwater Clean Detergent saying, "It lived up to the promise, vanquishing blood, chocolate ice cream, grass, and other tough stains in our tests." *Consumer Reports* took the added step in their 2014 article, cutely titled "Doing Laundry In Cold Water Will

Save You Loads," of inferring that users of cold-water washing detergents will recoup the cost of their laundry detergent this year through the reduced energy bills associated with the reduction in hot water consumption.[34] Their calculations are based upon the projected sixty dollar annual energy savings and a detergent cost of twenty-five cents per load. Assuming an average annual household wash rate of three hundred loads per year, the detergent cost would be mostly eclipsed by the annual energy savings associated with cold-water washing.

Drain Water Heat Recovery System

Slowly gaining popularity, these systems transfer the energy stored in waste water in the form of heat to preheat water en-route to your home's hot water heater.[35] A specialized heat transfer system pulls excess energy stored in waste water and transfers this energy to water on the way to your hot water heater. Preheating water before it enters the home's hot water heater using the energy (or heat) existing in the waste water reduces the amount of new energy that needs to be consumed by a home's hot water heater to bring it up to the user's desired temperature.

Ranging from $300 to $1500, these systems work either with a storage tank that holds preheated water until it is needed by the home's hot water heater or through a heat exchanger working in real time to transfer heat from waste water to new water being piped in to the hot water heater.

For larger families consuming a significant amount of hot water, heat recovery systems can help significantly reduce domestic water heating costs by recycling energy that otherwise would literally go down the drain.

Energy Efficient Water Heaters

Water heating is the second largest energy expense in your home and there is a multitude of types of hot water heaters on the market. Variables including climate, consumption, fuel, and lifestyle will all impact the type of water heating system best for your home.

Although typically more expensive, on-demand tankless units are worth looking into for families with lower consumption. Unlike conventional hot water heaters that store large amounts of preheated hot water in a storage tank, on-demand units produce hot water on an as-needed basis by using high intensity combustion to bring water up to the desired temperature quickly.

Also referred to as "hybrid" water heaters, heat pump water heaters transfer energy stored in the surrounding air in the form of ambient heat to water held in the tank of the water heater. During periods of high demand, this type of unit will engage its alternative conventional heating system to produce higher volumes of water.[36]

Homes in colder climates might benefit from an "indirect" style hot water heater. This type of unit uses the home's heating system to heat water for the household. With this option, coils of fluid heated by the home's heating system are circulated through the hot water storage tank. According to the U.S. Department of Energy, this can be one of the least expensive means of providing hot water when paired with a high-efficiency boiler.[37]

Tip: Similar to air-conditioning systems, heat pump water heaters simultaneously pull humidity from the surrounding air, making them good choices for homes with damp basements.

Tip: Drain a quart of water from your water tank every three months to remove sediment that impedes heat transfer and lowers the energy efficiency of your heater.

Ground Source Heat Pumps

The temperature a few feet below the earth stays at a fairly steady level year-round, and ground source heat pumps exploit this to ease the burden of a home's heating system. By utilizing the constant temperature of the earth to buffer heating and cooling days, the home's heating and cooling systems expend less energy to bring indoor temperatures to a comfortable range.[38]

For example, even during an extreme cold snap, the earth's temperature remains relatively steady. In New Jersey, it's approximately fifty-five degrees. This means that if the outdoor temperature is twenty degrees, the heating system gets a "head start" by cycling fluid below the earth's surface long enough to bring the temperature of this fluid up to fifty-five degrees. Once it cycles back through the home's heating system, the fluid only needs to consume the energy necessary to add an additional ten to fifteen degrees of temperature before being distributed throughout the home. This approach consumes significantly less energy than having to bring much colder fluid to temperature.

Home Energy Audit

Consumer Reports magazine says, "Unlike the IRS version, a home energy audit can save you money. It provides a comprehensive assessment of your home's heating, cooling, and distributions systems; an insulation checkup; and a review of your energy bills."[39]

During a home energy audit, certified technicians perform a top-down examination of your home to uncover opportunities to improve your home's comfort and energy efficiency. Comprehensive reporting provides the insight necessary to make important decisions about home improvement upgrades.

Consumer Reports also suggests checking with local utilities or other energy efficiency incentive programs to see if discounted home energy audits are available in your area. The website dsireusa.org, maintained by the NC State University through a grant from the U.S. Department of Energy, provides a listing of incentive programs around the country. They also recommend checking the credentials of your provider to ensure they are Building Performance Institute (BPI) or Residential Energy Services Network (RESNET) certified.[40]

Martha Stewart ranks a home energy audit as the number one item on her list of "52 Ways to Improve the World."[41] Martha's 1932 Connecticut cottage underwent an energy audit after they spent their first winter, "sleeping in fleece pullovers and ski socks – and with utility bills through the new roof."[42] So they signed up for a Connecticut program that helped diagnose where the home was losing energy and offered assistance with repairs and upgrades.

A home energy audit or home energy assessment is designed to uncover how a home loses or wastes energy. From the foundational elements of energy efficiency to incentives, pricing, and prescriptive improvements for your home, a home energy audit gives you everything you need to improve the comfort, safety, and energy efficiency of your home.

Power Off

The old adage "turn the lights off behind you" still holds true. However, throwing a few more switches will save bigger bucks. Cable boxes, televisions, monitors, computers, and other electronic devices consume large amounts of power even in standby mode.

With the advent of multi-room DVR's, there's no reason not to connect devices in other rooms to a power strip and flip the switch when you leave to save big on energy costs.

Line Dry Clothes

Need we say more?

Attic Hatch Cover

Warm air is naturally drawn to cooler spaces. During summer months, attic temperatures will likely reach extreme levels, buffered only by a thin flimsy piece of plywood on the pull-down stairs of many attics.

Erik North, owner of Free Energy Maine and *Green Building Advisor* contributor, says, "An attic hatch can have finished trim and paint, look perfect, and still be a giant heat sink. In the summers, it will radiate heat down into the house..." North suggests that, when adding an attic hatch, "the goal is two-fold: air sealing to prevent air-transported heat loss and beefing up the insulation."[43]

Installing an insulated stair cover in the attic will add significant resistance to one of your home's least insulated spots. Insulated stair covers can be purchased online or hand-crafted using polyisocyanurate rigid foam board. Either way, be sure to apply weatherstripping to the underside of the assembly to block any connection between your living space and the attic above.

Tip: No pull-down ladder? Polyisocyanurate is fairly easy to work with and can be applied to the back of walk-up attic doors and to the surface of a push-up attic hatch.

Outdoor Cooking

Isn't this what summer's all about? Keep the heat outside by cooking outdoors. Spend time with your family, laugh, have fun, and enjoy each other's company by sharing a meal together outdoors.

In their article "Unorthodox Summer Energy Saving Tips," the *Green Mountain Energy* blog suggests not limiting the grill to weekends or 4th of July holidays. Nick says, "Instead of switching on your stovetop or turning on the oven, which heats up your home, cook outside to make life more comfortable inside."[44]

The article also suggests taking advantage of summer's abundance of fresh fruits and vegetables by eating more uncooked food like salad, fruit, cereal, olives, and cheese to lessen a household's use of electricity and gas.

Outdoor Elegance, a California Patio Design Center devoted to "Bringing the California Lifestyle to Life," suggests that "perhaps the best place to get started is by creating a space in the backyard with plenty of space for family and friends to sit and gather around." They add, "If you enjoy eating outside then consider setting up the dining table to look upon the best view in the entire backyard. It doesn't matter if that view is overlooking something as grand as an ocean, or something as small as a garden; just make sure it is your favorite place to spend time & make memories."[45]

If your outdoor ambiance isn't compelling you to spend time outdoors, Outdoor Elegance suggests adding a "living wall" with plants and flowers, or mounting a few bird houses onto an empty wall to create an attractive focal point that will become "a wonderful sight that can be enjoyed on a daily basis."

Other ideas from Outdoor Elegance include adding a cocktail cart to make preparing and mixing drinks outside easy. Use trees to provide ambiance by hanging unique lighting pieces and add seating to provide a unique place to sit and relax beneath the trees.

Take Cooler & Shorter Showers

Being compared to cryotherapy, a hyper-expensive cold therapy that involves nitrogen and cold chambers, the popularity of cold showers is skyrocketing. The publication *Medical Daily* links cold showers to increased alertness, refined hair and skin, improved immunity and circulation, weight loss, muscle recovery, stress reduction, and potential relief from depression.[46]

In essence, cold water floods your brain with neurotransmitters that, in separate studies, have been shown to have a "significant decrease," in tension and fatigue and an, "improvement in mood and memory."[47] In essence, it floods the brain with happiness.

So, not only do cold showers save energy and feel great on a steaming hot day, but cold showers are also being associated with a myriad of health benefits and may sharpen your mind, firm your skin, soothe aching muscles, and reduce daily stress... Sounds good to us.

Outdoor Activities

Getting off the couch and into the great outdoors creates a huge reduction in the consumption of energy from all of the Netflix and associated devices that are not being watched, all of the social media not being consumed on an electronic device, the air conditioning that is not being used to cool the indoors, and the extra effort that your toaster oven, refrigerator, and microwave need to consume to nourish this bingewatching session. However, it's also great for your health!

The website Health.com links the time you spend outdoors to an improved outlook, improved focus, and a stronger immune system; this time outdoors may even help to relieve stress and depression.[48]

Business Insider takes it a step further, asserting that time outdoors may improve your short-term memory, restore your mental energy, relieve stress, reduce inflammation, decrease the risk of developing poor vision, improve concentration and focus, help you think more sharply and creatively, stimulate anti-cancer proteins, boost your immune system, improve your mental health, and reduce risk of early death.[49]

That's good enough for us.

Take Off Your Clothes

Wearing fewer clothes lessens the burden on your air-conditioning system to produce an environment capable of competing with extreme outdoor temperatures and layers of clothing being worn by indoor occupants. In fact, there are scientific benefits to shedding all of your clothes and spending time in the nude.

A recent *Men's Health* article points to a study performed by the National Institue of Child Health and Development and Stanford University, which studied 500 men who wore boxers during the day and slept in the nude at night. These men had a twenty-five percent lower rate of damaged DNA in their sperm than men who wore tighter underwear all day and night. Nude sleepers were also found to be happier in their relationships, sleeping better, having lower blood pressure, and burning more fat (specifically brown fat) during their daily activities.[50]

Not to be left out, woman's magazine *Cosmopolitan* says that sleeping in the nude is equally beneficial for women, as skipping the underwear removes the "warm, moist breeding ground for the bacteria that causes infections... and reduces the ability of those bacteria to overwhelm the normal healthy vaginal flora."[51] *Cosmopolitan* also links sleeping naked to healthier skin and hair and quite possibly a better sex life!

In a recent *Today Show* article, Dr. Lance Brown, a dermatologist in New York City, was quoted as saying, "Wearing restrictive clothing can cause excessive sweating, which may lead to inflammation of the skin follicles, rashes and breakouts. Going bare gives your skin a chance to breathe."[52]

Open the Windows

According to the U.S. Environmental Protection Agency, inadequate ventilation can increase indoor pollutant levels by failing to bring in enough outdoor air to dilute emissions from indoor sources and trapping air pollutants in the home.[53] High temperature and humidity levels can also increase concentrations of some pollutants.

The American Lung Association identifies a number of items that contribute to poor indoor air quality, including: asbestos, bacteria and viruses, building and paint products, carbon monoxide, carpets, cleaning supplies and household chemicals, dust mites and dust, mold and dampness, pet dander, radon, secondhand smoke, and volatile organic compounds or VOCs.[54]

Unless you suffer from seasonal allergies, in which case staying indoors with the windows closed and air-conditioning on is likely a better option, opening the windows will help ventilate your indoor space and draw fresh air from the outdoors into your living space.

According to Good Relaxation, fresh air is good for digestion, may help improve your blood pressure and heart rate, makes you happier, strengthens your immune system, helps to clean your lungs, and provides more energy and a sharper mind.[55]

Outdoor Entertaining

Outdoor entertaining can eliminate the need for air conditioning while providing a unique "al-fresco" entertaining experience. In a recent article, the Huffington Post had some ideas for adding enjoyment to your outdoor space.

Their first suggestion was to "deal with bugs" by screening in a porch. Other suggestions include removing standing water and changing standing water fixtures to running versions. Finally, they suggested installing a ceiling fan, which works to repel flies and mosquitoes while also helping guests feel more comfortable by circulating air on calm days.[56]

Other suggestions included the addition of outdoor speakers and the creation of shady spaces using freestanding umbrellas, cloth overhangs, lattices, and shade trees. Guests enjoying themselves in this environment are likely to be slow to leave, so make sure to think about the addition of solar lighting for guests that linger into the evening.

Blow Dryers

Just wash & go! Blow dryers not only consume enormous amounts of energy themselves, but the heat and moisture they generate add to the already burdensome task of the household air-conditioning system. In a recent *Vogue* article, stylist, salon owner, and brand ambassador George Northwood has the following advice: "I'd recommend having a longer cut with more of an undone feel to it – if your hair is longer, then it's less likely to spring up into frizz as the length weighs it down."[57]

The next step is to "really try to get most of the water out" with rigorous towel-drying. This will make hair a bit knotty, so a light comb will help relieve this, "but then don't use the comb again after that – you're trying to work with the natural texture."

Northwood recommends a bit of wave cream or curl cream, as these products are designed for air drying and will help to bring out the natural wave of longer, thicker hair. For fine or straight hair, Northwood recommends skipping the styling products in favor of applying a little oil at the ends to keep dry tips looking nourished and healthy.

Finally, Northwood suggests, "Just part it where you want and then leave it... The more you play around with the hair after that, them more you'll ruin it." Leave hair completely alone until it's fully dry. "Once it's fully dry, you can scrunch it and even add a little more product if you want."

Push Mowers

In "In Praise of the Push Reel Mower," The Art of Manliness, a blog dedicated to uncovering the supposedly lost art of being a man, authors Brett & Kate McKay purchased a Fiskar Staysharp Max Push Reel Lawn Mower to tend to the lawn of their new home. According to Brett, "This thing isn't your grandpa's heavy old contraption."[58]

We confirmed that, in fact, Fiskars used technology to improve the design of their eco-friendly reel mower. Winner of the Popular Mechanics Green Design Award and recommended by *Consumer Reports*, technology and advanced design make this push mower sixty percent easier to push than other reel mowers.[59]

A patent-pending cutting system allows the Staysharp Max to cut through twigs, weeds, and other tough spots that would jam other mowers while their exclusive StaySharp Cutting System allows blades to stay sharp. Brett says, "...it's given me the best mowing experience I've ever had."

According to Art of Manliness, push reel mowers are better for the health of your grass, make your lawn look nicer, don't emit pollution, and are cheaper, safer, and more fun than conventional mowers. In these days of paid gym memberships, standing desks, and Fitbit monitoring devices, a push mower is a great way to connect with nature, spend time outdoors, and work up a sweat.

In conclusion, Brett wonders why the manual push mower isn't more popular than the gas-powered variety. "It seems quite analogous to shaving. There are a few things where the classic turns out to do just as good a job (sometimes an even better one), and provides a more enjoyable and satisfying experience to boot... Give it a try!"

Swamp Coolers

During a heat wave in 1750, Benjamin Franklin was in his room, reading and writing with, "no other clothes on than a shirt, and a pair of long linen trousers, the windows all open and a brisk wind blowing through the house..." As he removed his sweaty shirt to change into a dry one, he noticed that the wet shirt he was changing out of felt cooler than the dry shirt he had in his hand. This moment prompted Franklin to try a series of experiments that led to the discovery of evaporative cooling.

The basis of sweating, this type of cooling is derived from a reduction in temperature resulting from the evaporation of a liquid, which removes latent heat from the surface from which evaporation takes place. Swamp coolers work by harnessing the cooling reaction that occurs as molecules, suspended in the air as they change from a liquid to a gas state, draw some of the latent heat from the surrounding air, cooling it down as the water and air find equilibrium.[60]

This type of cooling works much differently than a conventional air conditioner. With lower energy consumption, lower operating costs, lower installation costs, and lower manufacturing costs, swamp coolers are an attractive alternative to conventional central air systems. According to the National Association of Home Builders, savings generated through the use of swamp coolers total sixty million barrels of oil, preventing twenty-seven billion pounds of carbon dioxide from entering the earth's atmosphere.

The use of evaporative cooling systems in dry climates helps inhabitants re-hydrate dry skin and adds moisture to the air that can aid sinuses and other respiratory conditions.

Spare Refrigerators

According to the U.S. Department of Energy, twenty three percent of U.S. Homes have a second fridge, up from fourteen percent in 1978.[61] In a recent article, The *Washington Post* hypothesized that the "second fridge syndrome," as it is being called, is not only canceling out the energy savings from more efficient machines, but also contributing to a net increase in residential energy consumption in the U.S.[62]

In this *Washington Post* article, Steven Nadel of the American Council for an Energy-Efficient Economy says, "The typical second refrigerator might be fifteen years old when moved to the basement or garage, and might last five to ten more years there...Most second refrigerators are plugged in all year, but many are really only used for a few big parties, as well as to keep some extra drinks cold."

Using nearly twice the energy as their newer counterparts, that old refrigerator nullifies any energy advance that may be gained with the purchase of the newer unit, and to compound the issue, the older, less efficient refrigerator often needs to work harder when it is placed in an unconditioned garage.

California's Consumer Energy Center says, "One large refrigerator is cheaper to run than two smaller ones." Additionally, a full refrigerator retains cooler temperatures more readily than an empty one, another reason to ditch the "beer fridge" containing a few stray bottles of last year's skunk beer.

Drying Dishes

Instead of using the dishwasher's "heated" setting, open the dishwasher door and let them dry naturally.

In 2004, researcher Rainer Stamminger published the results of a study concluding that a dishwasher uses about half the energy and one-sixth of the water used by the average hand-washer. Stamminger wrote, "To clean the twelve place settings of dishes, the one hundred and thirteen test subjects used on average twenty seven gallons of water and two and a half kilowatt-hours of water heating energy."[63]

Another easy way to conserve energy is to allow dishes to air-dry rather than using the dishwasher's built-in heating element. In popular blog *Whole Natural Life*, author Meghan Slocum admits, "I'm all about green changes that don't require me to do a lot more work," and she tried air-drying shortly after moving into her new apartment, noting "I was happy to find that air drying was a huge success!" Megan continued, "When left to their own devices overnight, my dishes dried even better than the heated drying had worked on our old dishwasher. I've been air-drying our dishes ever since."[64]

In full candor, as Meghan provides, it's important to allow the dishwasher to fully dry, particularly during the summertime. The warmth, humidity, and food particles inside the dishwasher create a fertile breeding ground for mold and bacteria. In the rush of our chaotic lives, we mustn't have allowed time for the dishwasher to fully dry and we experienced some mold growth inside the appliance. We now alternate between the heating element and air drying.

Disposable Dishes????

Admittedly, this particular topic was an afterthought. Doing research for this book, I came across a blog post by Martin Holladay on Green Building Advisor's regular series, "Musings of an Energy Nerd." Martin's blog post begins with interesting information about the energy consumption of dishwashers, but evolves into a conversation about using china versus paper plates and cups, and which of these options consumes less energy.

As a guy who's been heavily involved with sustainability for a very long time and has spent an equal number of years constantly urging his wife not to purchase disposable products in an effort to reduce our household's contribution to the massive waste stream, the hairs on the back of my neck rose almost immediately at the thought of this question, and I found myself becoming a bit defensive!

In Martin's piece, he points out an analysis that compares the overall consumption of energy involved in both the production and use of a typical set of china versus simply purchasing disposable dinnerware. The analysis takes into account the energy consumed to produce the dishware and the energy savings yielded from fewer dishwasher cycles. The author assumes that the plates are made from recycled paper and the cutlery and cups from corn-based plastics that would biodegrade over time.[65]

Interestingly enough, the author of the study concludes there is an argument to be made for switching to disposable plates and bowls based upon a projected forty percent reduction in the amount of dishwasher loads. According to the calculations, switching to disposable cups and cutlery would likely not yield an energy savings and are, "probably out."

A separate study commissioned by the Dutch Ministry of Environment using Life Cycle Assessment/Analysis (LCA), which tracks the full life of a product or service from its birth to the end of its useful life, examined ceramic, styrofoam, and paper cups to examine the energy and water consumption that each vessel might consume over its lifetime as well as the contribution made by each item to air pollution and the solid waste stream.[66]

As it turns out, "with energy you'd have to use the ceramic cup six hundred and forty times before it would equal a polystyrene cup and two hundred and ninety-four times to equal a paper/cardboard one. Likewise you would have to drink one hundred and twenty-six and ninety-nine cups respectively for the ceramic to compete with polystyrene and paper/cardboard on the waste issue. And water? Sorry, just the use of a ceramic cup totals more than the entire life cycle water consumption of the other two."

Shocking, right!? Wait! There's a twist! The ceramic cup wins in the "functional use" category, which means that it can be used more than 3,000 times before it reaches the end of its functional life. So when durability gets factored into the equation, particularly in comparison to that of the "single use" cups, the ceramic cup is a clear winner. Phew...

Opening Doors

The U.S. consumes more energy each year than the rest of the world combined to keep our cars and buildings cool. Staying cool costs us almost a half a billion metric tons of carbon dioxide per year in pollution emissions.[67]

According to Allison Bailes at the *Energy Vanguard* blog, "An air-conditioner is a device that moves heat from one place to another. It picks up heat from inside your home and moves it to the outside."[68] In other words, it pumps heat from one place to another.

Today's air-conditioning systems use refrigerant that changes between liquid and vapor. The refrigerant enters the compressor in a vapor state. The compressor uses temperature and pressure to compress this vapor and pump it through the system into the outdoor condenser. This fluid and vapor is what travels through those copper pipes that connect the outdoor condenser to the indoor compressor. There, the condenser's fan cools the refrigerant as it travels through the outdoor coils. As it condenses, the refrigerant changes back to a liquid as the heat energy is removed and left outside.

In a nutshell, the system expends a lot of energy in its efforts to move heat from indoor spaces to the outdoors. Each time a door is opened, a rush of warm, humid air floods into the space and forces the process to repeat all over again.

Household Chores

In hot, humid climates, domestic chores like mopping floors and cleaning bathrooms are much more difficult to perform later in the day when afternoon heat and humidity are at their peak.

On her popular YouTube channel, "How Jen Does It," host Jen shares her tips on a quick morning cleaning routine that helps her streamline morning chores into 15 minutes. Starting with a typical morning, Jen takes us through her morning cleaning routine, which begins after her family has left the home.[69]

Need help? Becky Rapinchuck, author of *The Organically Clean Home* and host of the *Clean Mama* blog limits her homekeeping tasks to "fifteen to thirty minutes a day" and offers free cleaning calendars, recipes for healthy cleaning products, product tips, and daily inspiration to keep your domestic chores under control on her blog, cleanmama.net.[70]

Closing Doors & Windows

Mr. Money Mustache, a forty-one-year-old Canadian expatriate named Peter Adeney who runs mrmoneymustache.com, saved enough money as a software engineer in his twenties to retire at age thirty. He says about the energy consumption of his home's conditioning system: "For those without electrical engineering backgrounds, 3000 watts is an Absolute Shitload of electricity. It's enough to run two hundred and thirty modern light bulbs simultaneously."[71]

For those of us who alternate between air conditioning and fresh air, it's easy to overlook windows that aren't fully closed or latched. These can have an enormous impact on the efficiency and the effectiveness of your home's air-conditioning system.

Air conditioning works by continuously pulling air from the home's living space, separating heat and humidity out of it, then sending this air back to your living space. The consequence of an open window, particularly one located near a return duct, can quickly cause massive strain on your entire system.

We're big fans of the "Mustachian Way" of thinking about air conditioning, as Adeney describes in his article "How Not To Use Air Conditioning": "...as a pleasant luxury to be used when all other efforts fail. Much like a car. It should be an exciting moment in your household, when everyone is drinking their gallon-sized containers of ice-water, wearing comfortable and summery outfits of bare feet and tank-tops, and the ceiling fan is running, when you proclaim, 'God Dammit it is hot today!! Let's turn on the AIR CONDITIONING!! YEAH!!'" Love it.

Adjust Your Body to the Seasons

Dr. G. Edgar Folk, physiology professor at the UI Carver College of Medicine, explains in a recent article published by the University of Iowa Hospital and Clinic that the process by which you become physically adjusted to the temperature of your environment is called acclimatization and it plays an important part in how well you will tolerate heat and cold.[72]

Folk continues, "People who spend a great deal of time outdoors become 'outdoor acclimatized.' These persons are affected less by heat or cold extremes because their bodies have adjusted to the outdoor environments." When asked about how long it takes one's body to adjust, Folk says, "Acclimatization usually occurs over a period of about two weeks in healthy, normal persons. This process is faster in response to heat, but slower in the cold. Your physical condition, age, and other factors also affect how your body copes with heat and cold."

Folk suggests setting the air conditioning temperature ten degrees below the outdoor temperature, as "You may be better prepared to cope with the summer heat if the temperature of your indoor environment does not differ radically from the temperature outdoors."

Nutritionists suggest adjusting your diet to align with the seasons. The intake of local, seasonal produce helps your body maintain a natural transition between seasons.

Tris Thorp, lead Master Educator at the the Chopra Center for Wellbeing, suggests a cleanse to help rid our bodies of toxins, pollutants, harsh chemicals, and pesticides as a great way to begin the seasonal transition. Tris also suggests setting aside time for meditation, as it allows us to "...connect with stillness, to experience silence, and to acquaint ourselves with the ever present witness that is our essential nature."[73] At the end of each day, Thorp suggests introducing the practice of recapitulation which only takes a "minute or two" and allows you to "play out your day in your mind's eye and shift into the witnessing state of awareness, where it becomes possible to observe your choices and determine if there are any shifts you would like to make."

Blair Badenhop at the Parsley Health Blog agrees with Tris Thorp's recommendation to detox during seasonal transitions, and suggests adding yoga, cardio, and additional rest to maintain a healthy immune system and resist viruses and colds. Badenhop adds, "You may be surprised how incorporating at least one of the above tips into your life could make a world of difference."[74]

Air Movement

We love practical advice, so we're taking a suggestion from *Mr. Money Mustache*:

"...the temperature usually drops at night. So non-A/C users take advantage of this fact to open all their windows, and use large fans (100 watts) to exhaust heat and draw in cool air to chill air to chill the entire interior contents of their homes.

"A 100-watt fan blowing outwards from your highest window is pulling in night air from all other windows that is 10+degrees cooler than your house. By sucking in thousands of cubic feet of cool air per minute, this fan is doing almost as much cooling as the 3,000 watt air conditioning unit that does the same job during the day time."

Sounds like an easy way to create a nice evening summertime breeze through your home.

Bathroom Exhaust Fans

Keeping bathroom humidity levels in check is crucial during warm, humid summer months to prevent a myriad of unhealthy conditions—including mold and mildew.[75]

The first point we have to make is that if you have bathroom exhaust fans, use them. There's a significant percentage of the population that doesn't use the bathroom fan installed in their home or apartment because they hold the belief that not doing so will save energy. We've devoted entire books, blogs, websites, and social media accounts to ways homeowners can reduce their energy consumption, but in this case, skipping the fan is one of the worst ways to "conserve."

In fact, the more "energy-efficient" the home is, the more important it is to routinely utilize the bathroom exhaust fan for its intended purpose. Energy-efficient homes are tighter and less likely to effectively ventilate the humidity, smell, and pollutants generated in the bathroom. Without question, the combination of these ingredients will work together over time to spawn mold, decrease the indoor air quality, and potentially even cause physical damage to your home. In case we weren't clear: use your bathroom exhaust fan.

One of the easiest ways to put this on autopilot is to invest in a bathroom exhaust fan with a built-in humidity sensor.[76] This way, the fan will remain on long enough to fully exhaust all of the moisture remaining in the air, long after your teenage daughter's forty-five minute shower has concluded. Not only that, but the fan will turn itself on despite your daughter's objection to the fan's noise level. Programmable to specific humidity levels, these fans will manage your bathroom's humidity levels automatically, leaving you free to focus on life's other concerns.

Tip: Check to see that your bathroom fan is terminates outdoors through a roof jack or soffit vent. Exhaust from bathroom fans terminating in the attic is a known cause of mold, rot, ice damming, and roof damage.

Tip: SIZE FANS PROPERLY! There are easy calculations online; it's important to have a bathroom exhaust fan that's sized properly. A fan that's too small will struggle to exhaust moisture & pollutants, while a fan that's too large may affect other systems in your home, including its mechanical equipment.

Energy Efficiency Monitoring Services

We don't know what prompted you to pick up this book. Perhaps you've devoted your life to sustainability and energy efficiency, and as such, you are continuously working to reduce your impact on the larger environment—maybe. Perhaps you're like most of us, who have good intentions and work to incorporate sustainability into our lives when we can, and had the good fortune of having our book fall onto your radar. Whether it's the former or the latter, we can all use reminders along the way that prompt us to take action.

Recently, utilities have begun to offer interfaces allowing third party vendors to create applications that, with your permission, monitor your usage data. These applications allow you to add value to your utility data by offering suggestions on how to improve your energy efficiency and lower your energy costs. They also allow you to track your progress against historical data to pinpoint the effectiveness of your efforts.[77]

Companies like WattzOn offer personalized energy efficiency recommendations,[78] while other applications like Nest Mobile allow you to use their application to make changes to your system while away from home.

Utility Company Websites

Believe it or not, your utility provider's website can be a fantastic resource for energy-efficiency-related information. Utility programs range from cash incentives, free or reduced price home energy audits, and links to other resources in your community to complementary "tool kits," that often include light bulbs, power strips, and other valuable items.

Tip: Low-income individuals often have access to free or discounted energy efficiency products and services through community-based programs. Your utility's website is a good place to begin investigating these resources.

Incentives, Rebates, and Tax Credits

High-efficiency heating and cooling equipment is generally significantly more expensive than its less-efficient counterparts. Although this high-efficiency equipment will likely more than make up for the additional cost through lower fuel consumption, the high up-front cost of this equipment is often a major hurdle for homeowners seeking to upgrade their home's equipment.

A variety of local, state, and federal programs across the country exist to promote the installation of energy-efficient mechanical equipment. The most comprehensive listing of available incentive programs is the DSIRE website, operated by the N.C. Clean Energy Technology Center at N.C. State University and funded by a grant from the U.S. Department of Energy.

The joint U.S. Environmental Protection Agency and U.S. Department of Energy initiative, Home Performance with Energy Star, offers a national residential program that offers energy efficiency retrofits based upon standards developed by the Building Performance Institute. More than twenty-five states across the country have introduced retrofit programs based upon this model.[79]

Check online for additional incentive programs including those offered through local utilities, community groups, equipment manufacturers, federal tax credits, and non-profit organizations.

Opening Interior Doors and Air Vents

Air conditioning relies upon continuously conditioning and re-circulating the air inside your home. Many of today's homes have a centralized return located somewhere in the middle of the home. These returns, typically located in a hallway on each floor, draw air through the system and return conditioned air through the supply ducts located in each room.

If a room is kept sealed off from the rest of the home, it may feel cooler, but it might not be as comfortable as other rooms and will likely have higher levels of humidity due to the system's inability to recirculate the air from the closed room.

The feeling of resistance as you open doors to various rooms throughout your home is a simple way to tell if there's not a great connection between these rooms and your central return duct. Simple suggestions to improve air circulation within your home include trimming an inch or two off the bottom of doors, installing a transfer grille through walls or doors, or installing jumper ducts in the attic to help moderate the pressure between two or more rooms.

Tip: In tight homes, return ducts can become so starved for air that they begin to pull air down the chimney, drawing exhaust gasses back into the living spaces of the home.

Air Conditioner Maintenance

As Martha Stewart suggests in her spring checklist, you should have air-conditioning units serviced by trained and certified service providers. Just as any piece of mechanical equipment like your car, lawnmower, snow blower, and heating system requires regular maintenance and cleaning, your home's air-conditioning system is no exception.[80]

Many providers offer "subscription style" maintenance programs that will have your favorite HVAC technician returning on a regular basis.

Outdoor Awnings

In a recent blog post entitled "Using Shade to Reduce Energy Bills," home improvement expert Danny Lipford, host of the Emmy nominated television series, blog, and radio show *Today's Homeowner*, suggests that the installation of awnings over windows can reduce a room's temperature by up to fifteen degrees.[81]

The U.S. Department of Energy estimates that window awnings can reduce solar heat gain in the summertime by up to sixty-five percent, and up to seventy-seven percent on west-facing windows. The U.S. DOE website points out that, "In the past, most awnings were made of metal or canvas, which needed to be re-covered every five to seven years. Today awnings are made from synthetic fabrics such as acrylic and polyvinyl laminates that are water-repellant and treated to resist mildew and fading." Additionally, they add that "Choosing a light-colored awning will reflect more sunlight."

Door Sweeps

Don Vandervort of HomeTips.com, an online home improvement blog, describes a door sweep as "...a gasket that is fastened along the door's bottom face. It is made of soft material such as felt or rubber and presses tightly against the threshold or floor when the door is closed."[82]

In their blog post entitled "Small Actions That Add Up To Large Energy Savings for Earth Day," the American Council for an Energy-Efficient Economy notes that it is "...important to seal your home in the dog days of summer when your air conditioner is working hard to keep it cool."[83] They suggest adding door sweeps to doors to help seal up air leaks.

The U.S. Department of Energy calls the repair, "relatively easy,"[84] and we agree.

Power Settings

Today's LED monitors have dramatically decreased the amount of energy needed to display information from out desktop computers, but the computer itself continues to draw a significant amount of power to perform its tasks.

PCs offer more flexibility than ever before in selectable preferences as they relate to energy efficiency. In an article entitled "13 Ways to Save Power by Tweaking Power Plans in Windows" on *Digital Citizen*, author Mihai-Emilian Blaga offers a variety of suggestions including preselected power options including "balanced, high performance, and power saver" default settings.[85]

Blaga goes on to describe a variety of different power options located in the Advanced Settings section of the Power Options menu. These options include ways to save power while using Internet Explorer, selectively suspend power to USB devices plugged into your machine, and vary the power levels being used by the computer's processor. Other options include accelerating the computer's sleep countdown so it falls asleep faster, accelerating the computer's automatic display shut-off, and saving power when sharing media.

The most effective option is to completely shut down the computer for maximum energy efficiency.

Chargers and Fully Charged Devices

The U.S Department of Energy says the average phone charger left plugged into the wall with no phone attached continues to consume over one quarter watt of energy. A fully charged phone left plugged into the wall consumes an average rate of 2.24 watts of electricity.[86]

Sustainability blog *Eartheasy* recommends unplugging chargers when not being used, or plugging them into "smart strips" that shut off power to peripheral devices automatically when they are not being used. For the adventurous, *Eartheasy* suggests plugging devices into a Kill-A-Watt Power Meter, a device that gets plugged in between a charger and the electrical outlet to measure the phantom load of each device and charger so that you can concentrate your efforts on the worst offenders.[87]

When you consider how many chargers and fully charged devices are in the average household, it's easy to see how the combination of chargers, phones, and other "vampire loads" can add up to as much as ten percent of the energy consumption of the average household.

Lint Filters

A European favorite, hanging laundry outside to dry ranked dead last in a survey of one hundred and fifty different things Americans would do to lower summertime household utility bills. The Opower survey estimates that dryers rank among the top three energy-hogging appliances and account for six percent of the country's energy consumption, adding nine billion dollars to American families' utility bills.[88]

Opower writers Barry Fischer and Nate Kaufman recommend cleaning the dryer's lint filter after each load to improve the energy efficiency of the drying process. Additionally, the authors recommend "running the washer's spin cycle to remove excess water from clothes before they go into the dryer... and activating the dryer's moisture sensor, which prevents energy waste by automatically powering down the machine once clothes are dry..." as additional ways to save energy.

At the end of the day, Kaufman and Fischer suggest, "If you've never hang dried your laundry, summer is the best time to try it out. See what life is like without the tumble dryer for a week, and you're bound to see your summer energy bill tumble downwards." Worth a try?

Tip: If you are in the market for a new dryer, check out new heat pump dryers, which are popular overseas and are forty to fifty percent more energy-efficient.

Motion Sensing Lights

The energy experts at Saturn Resource Management estimate that automatic controls can save twenty to ninety percent on lighting costs.[89]

Brittany Bailey, author of *Pretty Handy Girl*, recently documented the installation of a motion detecting light on the rear porch of her home. In her words, "nothing deters a thief like a well lit area…but truth be told, I needed this light to illuminate the path when taking out the trash."[90]

Lights with motion detectors provide security and illumination when you need it, without the constant energy draw of full-time illumination.

Pool Pumps & Heaters

Energy efficiency expert Martin Holladay notes that "If your home has a swimming pool, your pool pump may use more electricity than any other appliance in your home – as much as three times the electricity used by your refrigerator."[91]

According to Holladay, "The typical California pool uses enough electricity during the summer season to power the average home for three months."[92]

The energy experts at Saturn Resource Management suggest using a timer to turn the pool pump on for limited amounts of time to keep the water clean. They suggest: "Try reducing this run time a little at a time and observe the water quality of your pool or spa for a few days. You might find that you need to run the pump as little as four hours per day."[93]

We love this advice, because the less the pump runs, the more you'll save.

Tip: Replacing older single speed pumps with newer variable speed pumps can yield up to eighty-three percent in savings over single speed pumps.

Tip: Pool pumps can now qualify for the Energy Star rating. Look for it when you buy!

Pool Cover

A recent study by Opower, an enterprise software provider, examined utility data from more than two million U.S. Homes, comparing energy usage between homes with pools and homes without pools. The Opower study found that homes with pools used an average of forty-nine percent more electricity and consumed nineteen percent more natural gas than homes without a pool.[94]

In the article outlining the study, author Barry Fischer dove further into the analysis to discover that pool pumps represented only about fifty percent of the increased energy consumption, which led him to investigate the cause of the remaining fifty percent increase. Fischer offered the following conclusions: "Homes with pools are bigger," with homes in this study averaging 2,052 square feet with a pool versus 1,693 without a pool; "Pool owners are likely to carry on a high energy consumption lifestyle," with pool owners averaging thirty to fifty percent more electricity in every season suggesting that "...behavioral differences that may go beyond maintaining a pool."

Fischer also found that "Pool homes have more occupants," which would equate to higher energy consumption, and finally, "Pool homes have higher income." This, along with data from the Association of Pool and Spa Professionals indicating that the "...median income for households with in-ground pools is $104,000 per year," which is roughly double the national median income, suggests a higher likelihood of additional televisions and other electronic appliances.

In his blog post, Fischer recommends that owners of pools use a pool cover, as a pool cover "keeps the pool water clean, which means that the energy-intensive filter pump doesn't need to run as much." Fischer also says, "a cover can reduce evaporation from the pool by more than ninety percent which saves a lot of water and keeps the water warmer." Without a pool cover, Fischer says the entire twenty thousand gallons of water in the pool can evaporate each year, and "refills aren't free."

Solar Pool Heating System

According to the U.S. Department of Energy, "You can significantly reduce swimming pool heating costs by installing a solar pool heater. They're cost competitive with both gas and heat pump pool heaters, and they have very low annual operating costs. Actually, solar pool heating is the most cost-effective use of solar energy in many climates."[95]

A solar pool heater works as the pump moves water through the filter and then through the solar collectors, where it is heated and returned to the pool. As an added benefit in warmer climates, the collector can also be used to cool the pool's water during summer months by circulating the water through the collectors at night.

According to the U.S. DOE, "collectors can be mounted on roofs or anywhere near the swimming pool that provides the proper exposure, orientation, and tilt toward the sun."

Refrigerator Temperature

Scott Cooney, author of "Refrigerator and Freezer: Ideal Temperatures and Humidities for Efficient Operation," suggests checking the refrigerator to make sure it is operating at the "most efficient level possible, while also treating your foodstuffs the way it should."[96]

Cooney recommends checking both temperature and humidity levels inside the refrigerator using a hygrometer, a device that measures both temperature and humidity and is commonly found inside humidors. If you don't have a hygrometer handy, place a thermometer inside a glass of water and place the glass in the refrigerator. Allow twenty-four hours for the water to fully acclimate to the temperature in your refrigerator.

The ideal temperature, according to Cooney, is thirty-seven to forty degrees Fahrenheit (four to five degrees Celsius). The U.S. Department of Energy suggests maintaining a slightly cooler temperature range of between thirty-five and thirty eight degrees.[97]

For your vegetable drawers, use the hygrometer to determine the humidity levels of your vegetable drawers. Store "stuff that will rot in the lower humidity drawers, and stuff that will wilt in higher humidity drawers." Leafy greens, broccoli, carrots, and green onions are good candidates for drawers with higher humidity, and grapes, mushrooms, and squash are good candidates for drawers with lower humidity.

Tip: Cover liquids and wrap foods stored in the refrigerator. Uncovered foods release moisture and make the compressor work harder.

WaterSense Faucets & Shower Heads

According to "Lower Bills with Low-Flow Faucets" on HGTV.com, "showers and faucets together use about twenty-three percent of an American home's water, more than toilets or clothes washing."[98] Replacement aerators and shower heads start around ten dollars, and the savings associated with these low-cost replacement options can be significant.

Low-flow faucets and aerators do more than reduce household water consumption; they also slow consumption of hot water and reduce the energy required to heat that water. In homes where the hot water tank is frequently emptied during the course of the frenzied morning rush and less motivated family members are left with a rejuvenating cold shower, these devices can add much-needed minutes to the morning routine. These devices reduce water expenses along with the expenses associated with heating the water.

Among the easiest energy saving devices to install, low flow showerheads and faucet aerators typically install with a few twists, and the savings begin the moment the device is fully installed.

The U.S. EPA's WaterSense program is a partnership that seeks to help consumers make smart water choices.[99] The certification program uses the WaterSense label to identify products that maintain high environmental standards without compromising performance. WaterSense branded products are certified to be at least twenty percent more efficient without sacrificing performance. Look for WaterSense labeled products when choosing new faucets or replacement parts.

Pipe Insulation

In Treehugger's online forum, "Ask Pablo," Pablo Paster is posed the question "Is It Really Worth Insulating My Pipes?" The respondent had a home energy audit performed on his or her home, and the accompanying recommendations included insulating the home's hot water pipes.

When posed the question, Pablo surmised that the primary benefits of insulating the pipes would include a reduction in heat loss of about four degrees, which would allow the home's occupants to turn down the temperature of the water heater by the corresponding amount. This reduction in temperature of the home's hot water would yield an energy savings that Pablo estimated would range between three and five percent.[100]

While the economics of having a professional install the hot water pipe insulation were unfavorable, Pablo took on the project himself in his own home and has already noticed some ancillary benefits; "These include the fact that the hot water in my pipes will remain warm longer between uses than without insulation (which is much cheaper than installing and operating a hot water recirculation pump) and that the sounds from my pipes expanding and contracting with the changes in temperature will be decreased, due to slower heat loss."[101]

Water Heater Temperature Settings

According to the U.S. Department of Energy, every ten-degree reduction in your home's water heater temperature will save three to five percent on your water heating costs. The DOE recommends that homeowners set their home's water heater temperature to one hundred and twenty degrees.[101]

Changing the temperature on the water heater to one hundred and twenty degrees is a simple adjustment that will likely go unnoticed by most other occupants of the home. Bear in mind that most hot water heaters are shipped from the factory with a temperature setting of one hundred and forty degrees, so this is an easy way to nail six to ten percent in savings on your hot water heating bill.

Leaky Faucets

According to Karen Wirth, the WaterSense marketing and outreach coordinator for the U.S. Environmental Protection Agency, "The average American family wastes more than ten thousand gallons of water and ten percent on their water bills each year from easy-to-fix leaks."[102]

To draw attention to what Karen calls "major water waste," the U.S. EPA developed "Fix A Leak Week," an annual campaign to generate awareness of this issue. Karen suggests checking your water meter before leaving home for a couple of hours. If upon your return, the meter hasn't changed, nothing is leaking! If the meter has changed, than you do have a leak and she urges you to have the leak fixed.

Karen offers another quick test for toilets: "Drop a few drops of food coloring in the tank at the back of your toilet. Wait ten minutes, and if color appears in the bowl, you have a leak. Don't forget to flush to avoid staining." Karen suggests that old or faulty toilet flappers are likely to blame, but are easy and inexpensive to fix.

For showerheads, Karen suggests, "Over the course of a year, a showerhead that's leaking just ten drips a minute can waste the amount of water needed to wash sixty loads of dishes!" If the unit needs replacing, Karen suggests trying a WaterSense labeled model, which can save twenty nine hundred gallons of water and seventy dollars on utility bills, and "the energy it takes to power your home for thirteen days every year."

Sounds like good advice to us.

Energy Efficiency Technology

Since George Jetson's flying saucer-like cars and robot housekeepers, we've been hearing about the "smart home."

A slew of technology is now becoming available, including devices like Tzoa, a portable environmental sensor that tracks everything from air quality and ultraviolet radiation to humidity and temperature. Set Tzoa on a side table and it will monitor the air quality of your living space. Clip it to your backpack, and it will display information about the surrounding environment and combine that data with that of other users to create a virtual pollution map.[103]

But the device with biggest potential to finally catapult smart home technology forward is likely the innocuous smoke detector. Thanks to Nest Labs, founded in 2010 by former Apple engineers Tony Fadell and Matt Rogers, a unique product gained traction with techies, environmentalists, and fans of good design. For the first time, a thermostat was on everyone's must-have list.[104] Casting an eye on the long-term, "internet of things," Google recognized the value of a device that could recognize the lifestyle patterns of a home's occupants, and had the vision to acquire Nest Labs in early 2014.

Since the acquisition, Nest Labs has been growing their foothold in the home automation market through its "Works with Nest" program that allows third party devices to communicate with Nest products, and for the first time in history, we're finally seeing a viable home automation platform come to market with simple but revolutionary technology. Nest works with everything, from water heaters that lower the temperature of a home's hot water when you leave and bring the temperature back up upon your return to "smart" carbon monoxide detectors that shut off heating systems upon and dryers that operate at lower levels to conserve energy while occupants are out.

It's still early, but if I was a betting man, my money would be on "Works with Nest" as the purveyor of automated safety, efficiency, and convenience functions in tomorrow's smart homes.

Weatherstripping

In their article entitled "The Benefits of Weather Stripping," *Home Adviser* says that air leaks can account for up to thirty to forty percent of the home's overall cooling loss, and notes that both older and newer homes have numerous cracks, holes, and spaces through which "unwanted hot air enters during the summer."[105]

The U.S. Department of Energy recommends choosing a product for each specific location.[106] Weatherstripping products are available in hundreds of different varieties, including different shapes, sizes, and materials. Identifying products specific to your individual weatherstripping applications will likely yield an easier, more durable, and more aesthetically pleasing application.[107]

Pay particular attention to entryways and attic access points. These areas are likely two of the biggest offenders, and addressing these areas can yield a significant benefit. While weatherstripping more complicated doorways, windows, and other penetrations can quickly become an advanced task that may be better left to a professional, it can also be one of the quickest ways to significantly improve indoor comfort and air-quality, whether alone or paired with larger air-sealing initiatives.

Task Lighting

Francis Rubinstein, a scientist and energy-efficient lighting expert at Lawrence Berkeley National Laboratory's Environmental Energy Technologies Division observes that "Study after study has shown that lighting systems which give a user personal control over the lighting in their work area results in saved energy. They give users who don't want the full level of ambient lighting the option to set lighting at the level they're comfortable with."[108]

One study by the Lawrence Berkeley National Laboratory concluded that the cost savings derived from the separation of ambient and task lighting systems may be as high as sixty percent for energy and almost fifty percent for life cycle cost.[109]

In their Residential Lighting Guide, Contech Lighting states, "...task lighting reduces the reliance on overhead lighting, and provides a better quality of light for specific tasks." They suggest "when lighting a task area, take into account the difference in brightness, or contrast, between the task area and the surrounding space. A 3:1 ration of task lighting to general illumination provides a nice contrast."[110]

Lighting manufacturer Dazor Lighting Solutions also notes that "ere is a renewed interest in task lighting." It is "'renewed,' because task lighting was all the world had known before our dependence on high-output overhead fixtures."[111]

Dimmer Switches

Dimmer switch manufacturer Lutron says that users who dim their lights with dimmer switches save energy as they increasingly reduce their lighting levels. Lutron claims, "the more you dim, the more you save." Lutron also says that dimmer switches have a built-in energy efficiency edge over their on/off rivals, and "Every dimmer automatically saves four to nine percent in electricity – even at the highest lighting levels – over a standard on-off switch."[112]

Lutron says that on average, dimming an incandescent or halogen light will reduce energy use by about twenty percent, and although incandescent lights are typically associated with dimming, "all lighting sources, including halogen, CFL's, and LED bulbs, can be dimmed."

Dimmers operate by reducing power to the lighting source or bulb, so according to Lutron, "Incandescent and halogen bulbs last up to twenty times longer when used with a dimmer." Lutron says LED bulbs paired with dimmers have the added benefit of running cooler when dimmed, "which can also extend bulb life."

Lutron offers the idea that there are "many ways to reduce energy use, most involve sacrificing something," and suggests that "dimmers and other lighting controls allow individuals to adjust light levels for specific entertainment options, enhance ambiance, set a mood, and take advantage of daylight to reduce energy use." That sounds painless to us.

Indoor Color Selection

Interior designer Jane Lockhart, principal designer at Lockhart Interior Design and host/writer of the long-running W series *Colour Confidential*, claims that "People don't always realize that paint color can have a big impact on their lighting's efficiency and how they feel in a room."[113]

Lockhart suggests using lighter, fresher color palettes throughout the home because "these tend to have more inherent solar reflectivity. They bring daylight into a space, so you don't have to use as many lights during the day. At night, they reflect more light around a room, so you need less lighting period."

An early stint at Benjamin Moore's paint and development labs gave Lockhart the technical background to pair with her natural eye for color. Lockhart suggests that consumers take the time to understand the specific LRV, or Light Reflectance Value, of the colors they are selecting. Located on the back of paint chips, LRV's rate a paint's ability to reflect light away from a surface. The higher the number, the more light is reflected. White paint typically reflects eighty percent of the light, while black paint typically reflects a mere five percent.

Lockhart suggests to clients in northern or rainy climates: "Paint your ceiling with white-grey with a tint of yellow – yellows have some of the highest LRV's. The combination will help brighten up your space by reflecting more light from above."

While she doesn't shy away from using dark colors, Lockhart does try to reserve them for rooms like bedrooms, basements, or dens that may get less use or warrant a "cozier" feel. When using these darker colors, Lockhart says that she may add special mood or decorative lighting to accompany these darker spaces and add a dramatic effect when clients entertain.

Exterior Color Selection

In "Summering Science: Can Your House's Color Reduce Your Summer Energy Bill?" *Scientific American* and Science Buddies offer an environmental engineering exercise to gauge the effects that color has on a home's energy-costs.

In the experiment, a white box, a gray box, and a black box are left in the sun with a thermometer inside each box. The readings for each box are taken and compared to another thermometer left in a shady spot. The black box had the highest internal temperature, followed by the gray box, with the white box having the coolest internal temperature of the three.[114]

The experiment is designed to illustrate the effect that a home's color can have on absorption of the sun's rays, and demonstrates the additional summertime heat gain that darker-colored homes will experience in association with the increased levels of heat absorption.

To illustrate the point of this, colormatters.com took temperature readings of a white, gray, and black roof on a sunny ninety-degree day in Austin, Texas. The white roof had a temperature of one hundred and ten degrees, the gray roof had a temperature of one hundred and forty degrees, and the black roof reached almost one hundred and ninety degrees. As the author points out, "under ideal conditions, if the attic is well ventilated and its floor heavily insulated, heat absorbed by the roof may be exhausted. Unfortunately, most homes have less than ideal conditions."[115]

Having had involvement in thousands of home energy audits, I can tell you from experience that most homes do in fact have "less than ideal conditions."

Refrigerator Door Seals

The California Energy Commission established the first standards for efficiency in refrigerators in 1976, standards that were eventually adopted by the U.S. Department of Energy in 1987. Since those standards were adopted, the energy efficiency of refrigerators has steadily increased by about two percent per year.

According to the California Energy Commission, "an average refrigerator today uses just twenty-five percent of the energy a 1975 model required, even though today's model refrigerator has increased in size by almost twenty percent and has features such as ice-makers and water dispensers." The combined savings of these efficiency gains save Americans about twenty billion dollars per year in energy costs.

On average, a refrigerator represents about thirteen percent of a home's electrical usage, still the largest energy-consuming appliance behind a home's air-conditioning system. The seal around the door of your refrigerator acts to keep refrigerated air inside the unit while keeping humid summertime air out. A quick check of these seals will ensure that the refrigerator is not working overtime to keep up with the air leakage and that your foodstuffs stay fresh inside your refrigerator for longer periods of time.

To check the seals, CA.gov's Consumer Energy Center suggests closing the door on a dollar bill and trying to pull it out.[116] If your seals are working properly, you should have a difficult time removing the dollar bill while the refrigerator door is closed. If the seals on your refrigerator door are not making a good connection to the body of the refrigerator, the dollar bill will easily pull out from between the door and the refrigerator.

Another test can be performed at night by placing a bright flashlight inside the refrigerator and directing the light toward different parts of the door seal. With the door closed and the room dark, look for light through the door seal.

If your refrigerator's door seal is found to be defective, replacement seals can be found online or at appliance-repair stores. Appliance-repair technicians can also perform this straightforward repair to ensure a proper installation.

Wash & Dry Full Loads

Blue jeans maker Levi Strauss & Co's "Unzipped Team" has researched the lifecycle of its legendary blue jeans, and their study "shows that nearly a quarter of the water used in the lifecycle of a pair of jeans comes from washing them in the laundry." Levi's goes on to suggest that, "By simply adjusting wasteful practices and replacing them with efficient ones, together we can help preserve our most precious resource."[117]

Levi's is practicing what they preach. As part of a larger movement towards sustainable business practices, Levi Strauss's Water<Less program was developed as part of a farm to factory push to innovate new ways to reduce energy, water, and waste at every step of production.

According to Michael Kobori, Vice President of Sustainability at Levi Strauss, "Our designers have challenged themselves to achieve the finishing effects our consumers love, while significantly decreasing water use." Kobori claims that "Levi's Water<Less program eliminates up to ninety-six percent of the water used in the process."[118] From recycling water throughout the manufacturing process to bleaching with ozone instead of conventional water and bleach, Levi's has saved over nine hundred and eighty million liters of water and recycled more than thirty million liters while crafting over seventy-five million Water<Less products.

Levi Strauss & Co is focused on improving the footprint of its products' entire lifecycle and has offered a number of energy-saving tips on its website, including many that we've covered in this book. Tip number two, "No item left behind," suggests, "If you must use a washing machine to wash your clothing, avoid washing only a single item. Washers use about the same amount of energy regardless of the size of the load. Be sure to load enough clothes so that you aren't wasting energy or water."

The Laundress is the self-professed "clean talk" blog of The Laundress, Inc, purveyors of an eco-friendly line of detergents, fabric care, and home cleaning products run by Gwen Whiting and Lindsey Boyd. The authors say to Load the Washer To Capacity."[119] Citing a study by Cambridge University that found that sixty percent of the energy associated with a piece of clothing is spent in washing and drying it and that a single t-shirt can send up to nine pounds of carbon dioxide into the air, they note that washing with a full load will use less energy than washing two loads on a low or medium setting.

Dryer Vent

Certified by the Chimney Safety Institute of America as a Dryer Exhaust Technician, Steven Schwaller and his Lincoln, Nebraska firm, "The Dryer Vent Dude," offer dryer vent cleaning and venting services. Schwaller's website cites statistics from the U.S. Fire Administration demonstrating that clothes dryers were involved in an estimated 15,600 U.S. Structure fires, fifteen deaths, four hundred injuries, and ninety-nine million dollars worth of direct property damage between 2002 and 2004.[120]

We compared these figures against the U.S. Fire Administration National Fire Data Center's Statistical Research paper entitled "Clothes Dryer Fires in Residential Buildings," published in January 2007, and found Schwaller's figures to be correct. Similar statistics hold true in later reports issued by the same agency.

"Failure to clean" is the leading factor contributing to clothes dryer fires in residential buildings. The U.S. Consumer Product Safety Commission recommends replacing plastic or foil accordion type material with rigid or corrugated semi-rigid metal ducts, and inspecting and cleaning them periodically.[121]

Although it pales in comparison to the potential safety hazards, dryer lint buildup also inhibits air circulation, leading to increased energy consumption.

Tip: Gas tumble dryers consume far less energy than electric dryers.

Washing Machine Upgrades

The American Council for an Energy-Efficient Economy's website, Smarter House, helps consumers make wise investment decisions about the products they buy, and offers advice on how to use them for maximum energy savings.

The Smarter House guidelines to buying a new dryer say that other than fuel type, the primary energy consideration is whether the dryer uses termination controls to sense dryness and turn off automatically. According to the website, dryers are available with two different types of sensors. One type senses moisture levels in the drum of the dryer, and the second type relies upon the dryer's exhaust air temperature to infer levels of dryness. According to the site, "Compared with timed drying, you can save about ten percent with a temperature-sensing control and fifteen percent with a moisture-sensing control." Additionally, "Over drying can reduce the life of clothes, so getting the timing right saves money in your clothing budget as well."[122]

Oven Temperature

In his Lifehacker article "Batch Oven Use for a Cooler Summer Kitchen," author Jason Fitzpatrick points out that older Southern homes frequently had two kitchens—one indoors and one outdoors. According to Fitzpatrick, "Summertime cooking in a kitchen with no air conditioning led those who could afford it to build a separate outdoor kitchen to keep the heat out of their homes."[123]

Fitzpatrick suggests that "there's no need to go to those extremes" and offers advice from a recent *The Kitchn* post entitled "Stay Cool! Make Your Oven Work Double Time," in which the occupants of an apartment offer suggestions on how to minimize oven usage during summer months.

With the exception of meat, the authors offer some good advice for cooking, including starting with the highest cooking temperature first. By batching items together, including baking two loaves of bread instead of one (one now and one for the freezer), and simultaneously roasting a bunch of beets while they were at it, they were able to save time. While the oven was cooling down, they toasted some nuts for salads and baked a half-batch of cookies. By planning ahead and cooking these items simultaneously, the couple minimized the heat gain created by the oven, both saving energy and increasing their overall comfort.[124]

The couple suggests cooking foods within like temperature ranges together and notes that most foods can be adjusted up or down by twenty-five degrees without significantly changing how they cook. Since the oven takes a long time to cool, they start with higher-temperature items first and gradually add lower-temperature items as they slowly reduce the oven's temperature.

According to the California Energy Commision's Consumer Energy Center, each time you open the oven door, the temperature drops by twenty-five degrees.[125] Recommendations include using the window with the oven light to check on food or using a clock or timer to cook food according to its proper length.

Tip: Some ovens hold heat for a significant amount of time. Try shutting off your oven between ten and fifteen minutes prior to the anticipated end time; the latent heat may finish the cooking process as the oven gradually cools.

Stovetop Cooking

According to Ben Morelli of the Yale Environment Review, cooking can account for 20% of consumers' total energy use. And food production as a whole constitutes 8 to 16% of the total national energy consumption in the U.S.

"The conscientious chef can chop energy use in half versus someone with more careless practices using the same equipment," says Morelli. "The simple practice of putting a lid on a pot during cooking can cut energy use by 8-fold," he adds.[126]

Morelli says the typical gas stove in America is only 40% efficient in comparison to its electric counterpart, which is 80% efficient. This seems straightforward at first glance, but Morelli suggests suggests, "Conversion from coal to electric by conventional power plants is roughly 30% efficient and can be as high as 40% when equipped with special devices. Natural gas plants can reach efficiencies up to 60%." This means that short of alternative energy sources, the most efficient conventional stovetop combination would be an electric stove receiving its electricity from a gas-powered utility plant.

Morelli advises that "Another best practice is to cook food in pots that are full to capacity. The efficiency of a pot is reduced by 80% if it is filled a fifth of the way. Cooking food in large batches takes advantage of the fact that boiling efficiency increases with pan size and volume of fluid."

If you're not cooking outdoors during the summertime, cover your pots and pans with tight-fitting lids. This will help the food cook faster while preventing excess heat and moisture from escaping into your living spaces. Additionally, you should match pots and pans to the burner size; pans too small for their burner will waste energy.

Stovetop Alternatives

According to the Yale School of Forestry & Environmental Studies, "The majority of studies reviewed agree that specialty appliances such as rice cookers and electric kettles 'consistently utilized less energy' than traditional alternatives."

Energy Star estimates that you can reduce energy consumption by as much as 80% by heating small portions in a microwave, and you might also have the additional benefit of air conditioning savings since less heat is generated when compared to using the stove or oven.[127]

In an article written by Rachel Sanders on Buzzfeed, Sanders suggests some innovative ideas including: using a popcorn popper to toast nuts; using the carafe of an electric coffee pot to cook vegetables and other foods; portioning pesto, stock, and tomato sauce using ice cube trays; using muffin tins as jumbo ice cube trays; using a slow cooker to cook dried beans and caramelized onions; using the freezer bowl of an ice cream maker to chill wine at a party; using a Keurig coffee machine to heat water for tea, ramen, instant oatmeal, or other things that need hot water; and finally, our favorite, using tightly sealed, heat proof containers to cook low temperature foods in the dishwasher as it cleans dirty dishes.[128]

The University of Connecticut College of Agriculture, Health and Natural Resources compared the energy efficiency of a conventional oven and compared it to that of a crock pot. They concluded that while crock pots run with lower energy wattage than a conventional electric oven, the conventional oven's heating element is only on for about twenty-five percent of the actual cooking time as it cycles off and on to maintain its temperature. They estimated that the total energy consumption between the two appliances was a toss-up, suggesting the comparative usage was probably "about the same."[129]

The comparison did point out that there are some newer, more efficient models of crock pots that had entered the market and may provide consumers with an energy efficiency benefit, and the comparative size of each crock pot would impact the efficiency calculations, with smaller crock pots being more efficient than their larger counterparts.

In the summertime, however, the latent heat generated by the slow-cooking crock pot will likely have far less impact than the full-sized oven would.

Dishwashers

According to the Consortium for Energy Efficiency, more than 60% of American kitchens have a dishwasher, and this appliance accounts for 2.5% of the energy used in a typical household.[130]

The California Energy Commission's Consumer Energy Center says, "Today's dishwashers use less than half as much energy and water as those made before 1994. Since almost 60 percent of the energy a dishwasher uses goes towards heating water, models that use less water also use less electricity."[131]

Dishwashers use almost the same amount of energy empty or full, and there is no additional cleaning benefit to running a partially full dishwasher. So load it up! The Consumer Energy Center says that "the savings will surprise you!"

The Consumer Energy Center also offers the following suggestions: use short cycles for everything but the dirtiest dishes, don't pre-rinse, avoid using the "rinse-hold" setting as it will use three to seven more gallons of water, and use the dishwasher's "air-dry" setting to dry dishes.

In regards to the question of dishwashing vs. handwashing, the prevailing opinion is that machine washing is much greener, but the answer depends on few variables such as the size and efficiency of your dishwasher, how you use the appliance (running full loads and using the light-cycle), and whether you let the water run while washing dishes by hand or fill the sink to wash and rinse.

The Energy Star program estimates that "Using one of their qualified machines instead of hand washing will save on average 5,000 gallons of water and $40 in utility costs each year, along with 230 hours of your time." That sounds pretty efficient to us.

Appliance Settings

Mister Sparky, the nation's number one electrical franchise, poses the question: "Do Eco Settings On Your Appliances Really Save Energy?" It's commonplace for manufactures of electronic equipment, computers, appliances, and televisions to include "eco-friendly" settings on the devices they manufacture. Eco settings can offer energy savings of ten percent or more, and according to Mister Sparky, the savings are "generally legitimate."[132]

In general, the Mister Sparky blog suggests that the reputation of a "few bad apples" may be affecting broader adoption of the use of 'eco-friendly' settings and offers, noting that "If consumers hear that the lowest power setting in a neighbor's dishwasher doesn't get the job done, they might be reluctant to try that option in their own unit, even if it's a different make or model."

Mister Sparky does acknowledge that there have been isolated reports of companies attempting to deceive energy testing measures, and that there have been reports of unsatisfactory performance of appliances operated under eco-settings, but suggests that the economy settings are usually included in good faith with companies preferring not to suffer the legal or reputational consequences of ill-performing products or manipulated testing.

With economy options being a standard option on most electronics and appliances, close examination of online reviews, coupled with additional research in publications like *Consumer Reports* and added emphasis on Energy Star rated products, will help consumers weed out poorly performing purchases.

Frozen Foodstuffs

Frozen or partially frozen foodstuffs will require longer cooking times. Depending on how these items are cooked, using the stove-top or oven will lengthen cooking time, adding additional heat to your home. Most packaged items including meat, seafood, vegetables, and other frozen items can be thawed in the refrigerator or in a bowl of water if shorter thawing times are desired. Microwaves are another alternative for quick turnarounds but are obviously less energy-efficient and may produce less than desired results by partially cooking the food.

A 2011 New York Times article entitled "A Hot-Water Bath for Thawing Meats" compared the thawing times of more than two hundred one-inch thick beef strip loin steaks. As part of a U.S.D.A. experiment to compare various methods of thawing times, the steaks were divided into three different groups—some in a refrigerator, some in sixty-eight degree water, and some in one hundred and two degree water.[133]

The refrigerated steaks took between eighteen and twenty hours to fully thaw, while the room-temperature steaks thawed in about twenty minutes. The steaks placed into one hundred and two degree water thawed in about eleven minutes, approximately the same time as a microwave using the defrost setting. The researchers added that the amount of time the meat spent in the water bath was so short that "any bacterial growth would remain within safe limits." On an additional note, "The water thawed steaks actually leaked less juice than the air-thawed steaks," and "no differences in tenderness was noticed between slow and quick thawed steaks."

Author Harold McGee noted, "So there's no downside to quick-thawing steaks, chops, fillets and other relatively thin cuts in warm water right before cooking. Large roasts are a different story." McGee points out that the extended amount of time it takes for larger roasts to fully thaw may allow for bacterial growth on the surface of the meat, and suggests that until further research has been done, "it's safest to continue thawing roasts in the refrigerator or in water under forty degrees."

McGee also noted that these studies were performed with the aid of an immersion circulator to keep the water in motion and at a constant temperature. In still water, "a cold zone develops around the food and insulates it from the remaining warm water. And without infusions of hot water or heat from a burner, the icy food cools the water bath." McGee suggests, "Unless I'm in a rush, I'm happy to let the letting the thawing proceed more slowly on its own while I take care of other tasks."

Sounds good to us; let's eat!

Kitchen Exhaust Fans

Use kitchen exhaust fans sparingly, as they pull both warm air and pollutants generated from oven and stovetop cooking and cooler air conditioned by your home's air-conditioning systems. To minimize the loss of conditioned air, run exhaust fans at lower settings to prevent large volumes of conditioned air from being pulled from the home.

A recent trend in kitchen design has been to install oversized commercial exhaust hoods in residential kitchens. These fans are rated to perform at much higher levels than what is necessary in a residential setting, and these oversized fans often create more problems than they solve.

Although they can be severe, the consequences of oversized exhaust range hoods have not been widely published. Building codes are adopting CFM requirements, but in most municipalities the CFM rating of kitchen exhaust fan falls through the cracks of larger remodeling projects.

According to Martin Holladay, oversized fans pose a problem in a residential setting because, "Every time an exhaust fan removes air from your house, an equal volume of air must enter."[134] As homes are built and retrofitted to attain higher levels of energy efficiency, the homes get tighter; this means fewer air leaks around windows, doors, and mudsills to provide replacement air for the volume of air exhausted by the kitchen range hood.

"If a house doesn't have enough random air leaks around windows, doors, and mudsills, the makeup air is often pulled backwards through water-heater flues or down wood-burning chimneys – a phenomenon called backdrafting." says Holladay.

During the course of retrofitting hundreds of homes, it's almost certain that a home with an oversized kitchen exhaust fan, operating at a high velocity post-energy-efficiency retrofit, will pull its replacement air down the chimney, drawing the exhaust of the unit into the living space of the home.

Coupled with other exhaust systems in the home, including bathroom exhaust fans and dryers, the negative pressure inside the home can reach levels significant enough to backdraft most chimneys. As a general rule, Holladay says, "most residential kitchens are adequately served by a 150-250 cfm range hood." The American Society of Heating, Refrigerating, and Air-Conditioning Engineers, or ASHRAE, limits exhaust fans to a maximum of fifteen CFM per 100 square feet.[135]

For comparison purposes, Holladay points out a GE Monogram range hood being advertised as, "lending elegance to any kitchen," rated at 1,200 CFM. According to ASHRAE requirements, the minimum size of a home suitable to install this fan without providing make-up air would be 8,000 square feet.

Fireplace Dampers

A fire in the fireplace is a great way to cut the dampness of early spring's cooler rainy nights. As the days and weeks pass by and windows are opened with the arrival of summer, it's easy to forget the damper left open on that rainy night weeks ago. During summertime, warm air is easily pulled down the chimney by the negative pressure inside your home created by air being pulled through the return ducts of your home's air-conditioning system.

On a sunny day, it's usually pretty easy to tell if your fireplace damper is functioning properly and offers a good seal from the outdoors. It's often possible to see daylight through a misaligned damper, and the 'feel' of the damper being closed isn't quite right. If this is the case with your fireplace damper and a proper repair is too expensive or difficult, a simple solution is to use a chimney balloon to create a more effective seal inside your chimney.

Matt Hickman of the Mother Nature Network calls a chimney balloon "a pillow of sorts," and says it comes in various sizes that will fit snugly either above or beneath the fireplace's existing damper. Hickman says, "Dampers are designed to prevent heat loss, but with age their ability to stop a fireplace's 'open window effect' is weakened. Some fireplaces don't even have dampers and repairing old/damaged ones can be a pricey endeavor."[136]

Hickman says that in addition to the chimney balloon's ability to keep cool air from escaping while the air conditioning is running, the chimney balloon can "keep pests, odors, toxins, debris, and other unsavories from traveling down your chimney and into your home."

Bathing

Recently, at a reader's request, the environmental news and commentary website Grist's Ask Umbra recently answered the following question: "I really enjoy taking long baths that use some lavender oils, etc., to relax on weekends and after work. How often (if at all) can we take baths in an environmentally friendly way, and are there certain products to use that are better than others?"[137]

Umbra suggests that "Showers almost always beat out baths in terms of water use," and estimates that the typical bathtub holds thirty six gallons of water, and would likely be filled with twenty to thirty gallons during the average bath. A longer shower with a standard 2.5GSM showerhead would not be far off of that mark, but "a more reasonable five minute shower using a 2GSM WaterSense shower head would use just ten gallons."

Umbra recommends being "frugal" with a bath, treating it as a special treat rather than daily hygiene, or rewarding yourself after performing gestures like "installing WaterSense faucets and toilets or a high-efficiency washing machine...,"[138] which would lower the home's overall water consumption.

Another alternative offered by Umbra is to collect the wastewater from baths, showers, and laundry for other uses such as irrigating your plants. A bucket or hose siphoning system could help with transferring water from the bath to the plants. If you plan to re-purpose your bath's greywater, Umbra recommends checking out the Ecology Center's, "Guide to Greywater-Compatible Cleaning Products,"[138] or visiting the Environmental Working Group's "Skin Deep"[139] cosmetics database to investigate the toxicity of a specific product's ingredients.

Peak Demand

In the late afternoon of the hottest days, home electricity consumption increases to forty percent above average, according to utility software provider Opower. "That's the time window when the day's temperature is generally the highest and also when many people are returning home from work or school," says Opower blog contributor Barry Fischer.[140] The additional demand coming online between the hours of 4:00 to 7:00PM overlaps with the already high demand generated by commercial properties as they struggle to cool billions of square feet of office and commercial space during the hottest hours of the day.

According to Opower, to accommodate the additional demand on super hot days, "power companies typically obtain electricity from a system of backup plants, called 'peaker plants.' These plants, which otherwise sit idle, can be flipped on quickly to satisfy "peak" power demand (e.g. everyone blasting their A/C at once)."

"Peaker plants are generally old and inefficient, using gas-turbine or steam turbine technologies that have low fuel efficiency. And as a result, flipping them on entails high operational costs that can be six times higher than a comparable power plant. Peaker plants also have a poor environmental reputation – they are considered to be more polluting than similar power plants that operate throughout the year." says Fischer.

Reducing electricity demand during these peak hours will likely result in lower bills, as many utilities have moved to "peak" rate pricing, and can help lessen stress on the electrical grid and relieve the pressure on power plants to keep up with the enormous demand generated during these hours.

Shop Locally

Vibrant neighborhoods and bustling downtown areas can greatly add to the enjoyment of a happy home. Our house, located two or three blocks away from Franklin Avenue, the vibrant main street that runs through our hometown, tends to be the gathering place for friends and family before making our way on foot to patronize local establishments. From our local farmer's market by way of the quaint local neighborhood coffee shop with its sunny outdoor patio to our local eateries ranging from burgers and pizza to dressy upscale restaurants, our downtown area is the epicenter of the community.

Sustainable Connections, a Washington-based non-profit founded by local business owners working together with the goal of supporting each other toward a shared vision of a sustainable local economy, offers a myriad of reasons to shop local, including their Top Ten on their website, sustainableconnections.org

The number one reason, according to Sustainable Connections, is to "Support Yourself."[141] What they mean by that is that a greater portion of the money spent at small neighborhood establishments remains in your community and serves to strengthen its economic base. We found a study by Chicago's Andersonville Chamber of Commerce and Andersonville Development Group that examined the economic impact of ten local businesses against that of chain businesses in the area and concluded, "Of every $100 spent at local businesses, $68 remains in the Chicago economy, while of every $100 spent at a chain, $43 remains in the Chicago economy."[142]

Sustainable Connections also cited stronger support for community groups, indicating that on average, non-profit groups receive 250% more support from smaller business owners than they do from large businesses.

They also point to a variety of other reasons, including a 'unique' community, more local jobs, better service, stronger community investment, local prosperity, and a lower environmental impact.

Walking

In 2008, John Tierney authored a New York Times blog post entitled, "How Virtuous is Ed Begley Jr.?" In the post, Tierney discusses an assertion made by author and environmentalist Chris Goodall that in some circumstances, the environmental benefits of driving are better than that of walking. Mr. Goodall's claim is that, "Walking is not zero emission because we need food energy to move ourselves from place to place." he writes. "Food production creates carbon emissions."[143]

Mr. Goodall equates the greenhouse emissions connected with the life-cycle of a cup of milk, which Mr. Goodall drank to replace the energy he expended after a 1.5 mile walk, are just about equal to the emissions from a car making the same trip. Mr. Goodall goes on to suggest that if two individuals were making the same trip, then the car would definitely be the more planet friendly way to go. Ultimately, results would vary depending on the type of car and the kind of food you eat.

Tierney goes on to quote Michael Bluejay at bicycleuniverse.info, who says that walking is actually worse than driving if you replace the calories with food in the standard American diet and if the car gets more than twenty four miles per gallon. Bluejay suggests that a bicycle is the most efficient (in calories expended per distance) in comparison to walking or driving when comparing one cyclist on a regular streamlined bike.

The Center for American Progress picked up on the blog post and continued the conversation, referencing a follow-up study by the Pacific Institute examining the same theory. The study showed that walking ends up being more harmful only if the "walker's replacement calories come exclusively from top sirloin – the highest GHG emitter."[144] The study asserts a different view of the "typical American diet," factoring in a more balanced caloric intake, and states that walking one and a half miles on the average

American's diet would generate less than a quarter of the greenhouse gasses that would be emitted if the person drove the same distance.

The study's authors, Michael Cohen and Matthew Heberger, give a nod to Goodall's underlying message that meat-intensive diets are energy intensive and greenhouse gas intensive, but they take a broader view of the "typical American diet" and state, "But as shown by the estimated GHG emissions of the typical U.S. Diet, walking – even for a group of four people – makes more sense than driving a given distance."

In their follow-up article, the Center for American Progress takes it a few steps further, citing that the benefits of walking also include lower air-pollution, lower related accidents and deaths, economic benefits, and health benefits.[145]

Public Transportation

The American Public Transportation Association says, "Public transportation is one of the most effective actions individuals can take to conserve energy," citing statistics that public transit"far exceeds the benefits of other energy-saving household activities, such as using energy-efficient light bulbs, adjusting thermostats, or using energy-efficient appliances."[146]

The Association claims that public transportation use saves the U.S. the equivalent of 4.2 billion gallons of gasoline annually or more than 11 million gallons per day. These benefits translate into a reduction of thirty-seven million metric tons of carbon dioxide annually and result in 300,000 fewer fill-ups every day.

The American Public Transportation Association says, " If an individual switches from driving a 20 mile round trip commute to using public transportation, his or her annual CO2 emissions will decrease by 4,800 pounds per year, equal to a ten percent reduction in a two-car household's carbon footprint."

Public transportation has the added benefits of reducing congestion and travel time for millions of individuals worldwide, resulting in cleaner and healthier communities.

Idling

The Environmental Defense Fund says that for every ten minutes your engine is off, you'll prevent one pound of carbon dioxide from being released. Calling carbon dioxide the "primary contributor to global warming," they suggest that the benefits are significant.[147] Reducing idling can keep the air cleaner in our towns and communities, helping to alleviate pollutants linked to asthma, heart disease, chronic bronchitis, and cancer.

According to the EDF, an idling car uses between 1/5 and 7/10 of a gallon of fuel per hour. An idling truck burns approximately one gallon of fuel per hour.

Suggestions to reduce idling include: turning off the car if waiting more than ten seconds, warming engines by driving rather than idling, warming cabin interiors by driving, and restarting the car more frequently.

Tip: Run errands all at once (and bring a friend)!

Location of Ducts & Mechanical Equipment

In his Energy Vanguard blog post entitled "Case Closed: Get Those Air Conditioning Ducts out of the Attic," Allison Bailes refers to a recent NREL report on the subject saying, "The report Ducts in the Attic? What were They Thinking?, summarizes the research that's been done about putting ductwork in unconditioned attics and basically says it's about the stupidest thing we do in homes that do a lot of air conditioning."[148] Putting ductwork in unconditioned attics and having cold air travel across hundreds of feet of attic expanse is, "an effective way to heat up the conditioned air as it travels from the air handler to the conditioned space inside the home."

Is your home's air-conditioning system located in the attic? A significant comfort and energy efficiency benefit may be derived by insulating the underside of your roof rather than your attic floor. Bringing your air-conditioning equipment inside the "thermal envelope" of your home will likely improve the performance and efficiency of the mechanical equipment by reducing the temperature differential of the surrounding environment.

A "Ton" of Cooling

A "Ton" is a sizing increment that refers to the cooling ability of air conditioning systems. The higher the "tonnage," the greater the system's ability to deliver cooling. A typical window air conditioner would generally deliver less than one ton of cooling, while a small home central air conditioner would be approximately two tons, while larger residential units would be four to five tons.

The American Society of Heating, Refrigerating, and Air-Conditioning Engineers defines a ton of cooling as delivering 12,000 BTU's (British Thermal Units) per hour of cooling and says the term is analogous to the equivalent amount of cooling ice that would melt to perform the same task during the days before air conditioning was invented.[149]

Selecting the proper tonnage for your air-conditioning system is critically important to a successful installation. A system too small will be unable to deliver enough cooling ability to adequately cool the living areas, while a system too large will "short cycle," a term that refers to a system reaching the proper temperature ahead of its ability to remove enough moisture from the air.

A load calculation program called a Manual J will perform calculations that incorporate the size and characteristics of your home to provide you with a properly sized unit that will effectively condition your living spaces.

Outdoor Central Air Conditioning Condensers

To allow for adequate airflow around the condenser unit, the U.S. Department of Energy suggests trimming foliage back at least two feet.[150] Dryer vents, falling leaves, and lawn clippings are all sources of potential dirt and debris, and should be minimized near the unit.

Opinions on the importance of shading outdoor condenser units vary with savings estimates ranging from two to ten percent. The U.S. Environmental Protection Agency has recommended shading of these units as a method to reduce energy consumption, but a Florida Solar Energy Center study that examined the effects of isolated shading of residential air conditioning condenser units generated only modest returns of less than three percent. The study suggested that the volume of air drawn into the outdoor condenser greatly exceeded the nearby shaded air volume, and suggested that greater savings may be realized by larger site and neighborhood-level landscaping that might be more effective at lowering localized air temperatures.[151]

Thermal Envelope

The National Renewable Energy Laboratory defines the thermal envelope of the home as, "everything about the house that serves to shield the living space from the outdoors. It includes the wall and roof assemblies, insulation, air-vapor retarders, windows, and weather stripping and caulking."[152]

To envision a proper thermal envelope, imagine taking a thick permanent marker and drawing a line around the silhouette of your home. The line should be continuous and contiguous, as should your home's thermal envelope. John Krigger, author of Residential Energy says, "The conditioned space should have a thermal boundary surrounding it, where insulation and an air barrier are located."[153]

An analysis and thorough inspection of the thermal boundary is one of the most effective starting points towards energy efficiency improvements. A professional energy auditor will perform a detailed inspection of your home's thermal envelope and help to develop a strategy for adding insulation and sealing air leaks in the chosen thermal barrier.

Air-Sealing Methods

Simple air-sealing methods include caulking around windows, doors, flooring, molding, seams, gaps, and penetrations in the thermal envelope of the home. A wide variety of caulk and sealants are available for both specific applications and general applications around the interior and exterior of the home.

Larger gaps in the thermal envelope can be addressed using expandable spray foam products and weatherstripping. Use caution when working near chimneys or other exhaust mechanisms for mechanical equipment as these areas require products rated for these applications.

A wide variety of specialty products is available at home improvement outlets and from online vendors. Pay particular attention to penetrations in the floor of your attic and along the sill of your basement, as these areas often represent the bulk of the air-leakage in a home.

Ventilation

"Either air leakage or a whole-house ventilation systems must provide acceptable indoor air quality,"says John Krigger, author of Residential Energy. "The American Society of Heating, Refrigeration, and Air Conditioning Engineers sets minimum ventilation requirements to maintain acceptable indoor air quality in homes."[154]

The minimum ventilation requirements typically depend upon the climate, number of occupants, and building volume. A device called a blower door is used to measure natural air-leakage to determine if the natural leakiness of a home provides sufficient ventilation, or if the installation of mechanical ventilation is required. Older standards recognized a home's natural leakiness as a ventilation strategy, but newer standards require the installation of a whole-house ventilation system to exhaust pollutants from indoor air.

The Building Performance Institute recommends that the air inside your home exchange to the outdoors at a measured rate of .35 times per hour. At this rate, roughly one third of the air in your home would be exhausted through the natural leakiness of your home. Many older homes exchange air to the outdoors at rates two, three, and four times these recommended levels which contribute to higher energy loss and higher heating and cooling costs.

Today's building codes place stronger emphasis on energy efficiency, requiring builders to construct tighter and more energy efficient homes. The natural tightness of these homes places added importance on mechanical ventilation along with proper usage of exhaust ventilation.

Moisture Management

Joseph Lstiburek of the Building Science Corporation says, "Moisture accumulates when the rate of moisture entry into an assembly exceeds the rate of moisture removal. When moisture accumulation exceeds the ability of the assembly materials to store the moisture without significantly degrading performance or long-term service live, problems result."[155]

Moisture management is generally comprised of controlling the entry of moisture into the living spaces, controlling the accumulation within the living spaces, and the removal of moisture from the living spaces. "Building assemblies in all climates can get wet from the exterior in similar manner by liquid flow (rain and groundwater as moisture sources). According,y, techniques for the control of liquid flow are similar in all climates and are interchangeable," says Lstiburek. He continues, "However, buiding assemblies get wet by air movement and vapor diffusion in a different manner depending on climate and time of year. Accordingly, techniques for the control of air movement and vapor diffusion can be different based on climate and may not be interchangeable."

The impacts of high inward flows of moisture are manifested as elevated energy costs due to high cooling loads, building fabric deterioration from decay and corrosion, and health and safety concerns from mildew and mildew growth.

Daily Routine

Minor changes to our daily routines can have a significant impact on our overall energy consumption. Simple changes like adding standing water to the sink while shaving, rather than a constant stream of running water can add up to thousands of gallons over time.

The addition of simple behavioral items like many of the ones discussed in this book will have an enormous collective impact on energy consumption if widely adopted. Raising temperature set-points can be as impactful as installing all new windows.

Technology is also delivering more and more automation to the energy efficiency space and providing more insight on the individual benefits of these actions. This sword swings both ways however, as energy efficiency gains are being offset by the construction of larger homes and a broadening array of electronic devices.[156]

1Notes

Alyson McNutt English, "Guide to Energy-Efficient Window Coverings," *House Logic*, accessed June 2016. https://www.houselogic.com/remodel/windows-doors-and-floors/save-money-energy-efficient-window-coverings/

2Hunter Douglas Contract, *Window Coverings Brochure* (Poway, CA: Hunter Douglas International, 2009). http://www.hunterdouglasarchitectural.com/documents/windowCoverings/CWC_Brochure.pdf

3"Energy-Efficient Window Treatments," Energy.Gov, accessed June 2016. http://energy.gov/energysaver/energy-efficient-window-treatments

4John Krigger, *Residential Energy: Cost Savings and Comfort for Existing Buildings (6th Edition)* (New York: Pearson, 2013).

5"Window Films," *3M*, accessed June 2016. http://solutions.3m.com/wps/portal/3M/en_US/Window_Film/Solutions/

6"Energy Efficient Windows: What You Need to Know," *RESNET*, April 17, 2012. http://www.resnet.us/library/energy-efficient-windows-what-you-need-to-know/

7Energysaver.gov, *Energy Saver: Tips on Saving Money and Energy at Home* (Washington, D.C: U.S. DOE, 2014). http://energy.gov/sites/prod/files/2014/09/f18/61628_BK_EERE-EnergySavers_w150.pdf

8"LED: Revolutionary Lighting," *Living on Earth*, accessed June 2016. http://loe.org/series/series.html?seriesID=16

9Richard Wilson, "Why LED Lighting Is So Important to the Chip Market," *ElectronicsWeekly.com,* January 27, 2016. http://www.electronicsweekly.com/news/why-led-lighting-is-so-important-to-the-chip-market-2016-01/

10"OLED Lighting: introduction and market status," *OLED-info,* accessed June 2016. http://www.oled-info.com/oled-light

11"LG Displays flexible OLED at Light+Building 2016," *Lighting Inspiration*, April 11, 2016. http://www.lighting-inspiration.com/lg-dislay-oled-light-building-2016/

12Mariana Pickering, "6 Busted Green Roof Myths," *Forbes,* December 30, 2013. http://www.forbes.com/sites/houzz/2013/12/30/6-busted-green-roof-myths/2/#46389d94421f

13 US DOE, *Landscaping for Energy Efficiency* (Washington, DC: NREL, 1995).

14"How to Plant Trees to Conserve Energy for Summer Shade," Arbor Day Foundation, accessed June 2016. https://www.arborday.org/trees/climatechange/summershade.cfm

15Terry Carter, "Create an Energy Efficient Garden," Earth Times, August 15, 2012. http://www.earthtimes.org/green-blogs/green-living/create-energy-efficient-garden-15-Aug-12/

16Jennifer Stimpson, "How to Build a Trellis," *This Old House Magazine,* accessed June 2016. http://www.thisoldhouse.com/toh/how-to/intro/0,,20269959,00.html

17Kilian Ganly, "Trellis Training Tips," *Right@Home*, accessed June 2016. http://www.rightathome.com/Designing/OutdoorLiving/Pages/TrellisTrainingTips.aspx#

18Lindsey Turrentine, "Nest Learning Thermostat Review," CNET, updated April 29, 2013. http://www.cnet.com/products/nest-learning-thermostat/

19"Works With Nest," Nest Labs, accessed June 2016. https://nest.com/works-with-nest/

20Jean Nick, "How to Keep Your House Cool Without AC," *Rodale's Organic Life*, July 13, 2015. http://www.rodalesorganiclife.com/home/how-keep-your-house-cool-without-ac

21Martin Holladay, "Sealing Ducts: What's Better, Tape or Mastic?" *Musings of an Energy Nerd,* August 6, 2010. http://www.greenbuildingadvisor.com/blogs/dept/musings/sealing-ducts-what-s-better-tape-or-mastic

22"Tips: Air Ducts," Energy.Gov, accessed June 2016. http://energy.gov/energysaver/tips-air-ducts

23"Central Air Conditioning Buying Guide," *Consumer Reports*, April 2016. http://www.consumerreports.org/cro/central-air-conditioning/buying-guide.htm

24O'Brien Service Company, "How Often Should You Replace Your Home Air Filter?" Angie's List, November 13, 2015. https://www.angieslist.com/articles/how-often-should-you-replace-your-home-air-filter.htm

25"Technically Speaking: Principles of Heat Transfer," Building Performance Institute, Inc., March 11, 2016. http://www.bpihomeowner.org/blog/technically-speaking-principles-heat-transfer

26"Where to Insulate in a Home," Energy.Gov, accessed June 2016. http://energy.gov/energysaver/where-insulate-home

27"Vast Majority of U.S. Homes Are Under Insulated," *RESNET*, December 8, 2015. http://www.resnet.us/library/vast-majority-u-s-homes-insulated/

28Martin Holladay, "How to Insulate a Basement Wall," *Musings of an Energy Nerd*, June 29, 2012. http://www.greenbuildingadvisor.com/blogs/dept/musings/how-insulate-basement-wall

29Tom Harrison, Jr., "How an Energy Audit, Some Caulk and Insulation (Total Cost $1175) is Saving Me $1000…Per Year," Energy Circle, January 22, 2010. http://www.energycircle.com/blog/2010/01/22/how-an-energy-audit-some-caulk-and-insulation-total-cost-1175-is-saving-me-

1000-per-year

30"Certified Products," Energy Star, accessed June 2016.
https://www.energystar.gov/products

31"Efficient Laundry: Wash Clothes in Cold Water to Save
Energy," Alliance to Save Energy, October 5, 2011.
https://www.ase.org/resources/efficient-laundry-wash-clothes-
cold-water-save-energy

32Andrew Martin and Elisabeth Rosenthal, "Cold-Water
Detergents Get a Cold Shoulder," *New York Times*, September 16,
2011. http://www.nytimes.com/2011/09/17/business/cold-water-
detergents-get-a-chilly-reception.html?_r=3&pagewanted=all

33"Sustainability Reports," Procter & Gamble Co., accessed June
2016.
http://www.pg.com/en_US/sustainability/performance/index.shtm
l

34"Doing laundry in cold water will save you loads," *Consumer
Reports*, October 31, 2014.
http://www.consumerreports.org/cro/news/2014/10/doing-
laundry-in-cold-water-will-save-you-loads/index.htm

35"Drain-Water Heat Recovery," Energy.Gov, accessed June
2016. http://energy.gov/energysaver/drain-water-heat-recovery

36"How it Works—Heat Pump Water Heaters," Energy Star,
accessed June 2016.

https://www.energystar.gov/products/water_heaters/high_efficiency_electric_storage_water_heaters/how_it_works

37"Tankless Coil and Indirect Water Heaters," Energy.Gov, accessed June 2016. http://energy.gov/energysaver/tankless-coil-and-indirect-water-heaters

38"Geothermal Heat Pumps," Energy.Gov, accessed June 2016. http://energy.gov/energysaver/geothermal-heat-pumps

39"Good news: You're being audited!" *Consumer Reports*, October 2009. http://www.consumerreports.org/cro/magazine-archive/october-2009/home-garden/cut-your-energy-bills/you-are-being-audited/cut-your-energy-bills-being-audited.htm

40"Database of State Incentives for Renewables & Efficiency," DSIRE, accessed June 2016. http://www.dsireusa.org/

41"52 Ways to Improve the World," MarthaStewart.com, accessed June 2016. http://www.marthastewart.com/270414/52-ways-to-improve-the-world

42"Anatomy of a Drafty House," MarthaStewart.com, accessed June 2016. http://www.marthastewart.com/852356/anatomy-drafty-house

43Erik North, "How to Insulate and Air Seal an Attic Hatch," Green Building Advisor, May 2, 2012. http://www.greenbuildingadvisor.com/blogs/dept/guest-blogs/how-insulate-and-air-seal-attic-hatch

44 Nick, "Unorthodox Summer Energy-Saving Tips," *Green Mountain* Blog, updated December 29, 2014. https://www.greenmountainenergy.com/2014/08/unorthodox-summer-energy-saving-tips/

45 Thomas Kay, "25 Patio Decorating Tips and Design Ideas to Transform Your Backyard," *Outdoor Living & Lifestyle Blog*, May 28, 2015. http://blog.outdoorelegance.com/topic/outdoor-entertaining

46 Lizette Borreli, "Benefits of Cold Showers: 7 Reasons Why Taking Cool Showers Is Good For Your Health," *Medical Daily*, June 24, 2014. http://www.medicaldaily.com/benefits-cold-showers-7-reasons-why-taking-cool-showers-good-your-health-289524

47 Chris Gayomali, "The Scientific Case For Cold Showers," *My Creative Life*, March 18, 2015. http://www.fastcompany.com/3043767/my-creative-life/the-scientific-case-for-cold-showers

48 Chloe Metzger, "5 (Scientific!) Reasons Getting Outside is Good for You," *Health Magazine*, September 29, 2014. http://news.health.com/2014/09/29/health-benefits-of-nature/

49 Lauren F. Friedman and Kevin Loria, "11 scientifically proven reasons you should be spending less time in the office," *Business Insider*, June 30, 2015. http://www.businessinsider.com/why-being-outside-in-nature-is-healthy-2015-6

50 Brittany Smith, "5 Benefits of Sleeping Naked," *Men's Fitness*, accessed June 2016.
http://www.mensfitness.com/life/4-benefits-sleeping-naked

51 Hannah Smothers, "6 Reasons You Should Sleep Naked," *Cosmopolitan*, April 28, 2016.
http://www.cosmopolitan.com/health-fitness/g2681/sleep-naked/

52 Jordi Lippe-McGraw, "The health benfits of being naked: how stripping down is good for you," *Today*, September 25, 2015.
http://www.today.com/health/health-benefits-being-naked-how-stripping-down-good-you-t44911

53 "Protect Indoor Air Quality in Your Home," EPA, accessed June 2015. https://www.epa.gov/indoor-air-quality-iaq/protect-indoor-air-quality-your-home#tab-1

54 "Ventilation: How Buildings Breathe," American Lung Association, accessed June 2016. http://www.lung.org/our-initiatives/healthy-air/indoor/at-home/ventilation-buildings-breathe.html

55 Urmet Seepter, "6 Health Benefits of Fresh Air," Good Relaxation, January 3, 2012.
http://goodrelaxation.com/2012/01/health-benefits-of-fresh-air/

56 Laura Gaskill, "How to Enjoy Your Outdoor Space More," *The Huffington Post*, July 2, 2015.

http://www.huffingtonpost.com/Houzz/how-to-enjoy-your-outdoor_b_7717158.html

57Lisa Niven, "A Guide To Air-Drying Your Hair," *Vogue*, March 28, 2016. http://www.vogue.co.uk/beauty/2014/06/19/how-to-air-dry-your-hair-for-summer-by-george-northwood

58Brett and Kate McKay, "In Praise of the Push Reel Mower," The Art of Manliness, May 23, 2012. http://www.artofmanliness.com/2012/05/23/in-praise-of-the-push-reel-mower/

59"StaySharp^{TM} Max Reel Mower," Fiskars, accessed June 2016. http://www2.fiskars.com/Products/Gardening-and-Yard-Care/Reel-Mowers/StaySharp-Max-Reel-Mower

60 Chris Landers, "How Swamp Coolers Work," HowStuffWorks.com, accessed June 2016. http://home.howstuffworks.com/home-improvement/heating-and-cooling/swamp-cooler3.htm

61 "Department of Energy," Energy.Gov, accessed June 2016. energy.gov

62Chris Mooney, "Why it's not okay to have a second refrigerator," *The Washington Post*, November 26, 2014. https://www.washingtonpost.com/news/wonk/wp/2014/11/26/why-its-not-okay-to-have-a-second-refrigerator/

63Rainer Stamminger, "Is a Machine More Efficient Than the Hand?" *Home Energy Magazine*, May 1, 2004. http://homeenergy.org/show/article/page/9/id/180

64Meghan Slocum, "Save Energy by Letting Your Dishwasher Air Dry," *Whole Natural Life*, December 14, 2012. http://wholenaturallife.com/save-energy-by-letting-your-dishwasher-air-dry/

65Martin Holladay, "All About Dishwashers," *Musings of an Energy Nerd*, June 14, 2013. http://www.greenbuildingadvisor.com/blogs/dept/musings/all-about-dishwashers

66"EcoTip: Coffee cups-spilling the beans," Treehugger, November 19, 2004. http://www.treehugger.com/culture/ecotip-coffee-cups-spilling-the-beans.html

67Stan Cox, "Climate risks heat up as world switches on to air conditioning," *The Guardian*, July 10, 2012. http://www.theguardian.com/environment/2012/jul/10/climate-heat-world-air-conditioning

68Allison Bailes, "The Magic of Cold, Part 1-How Your Air Conditioner Works," *Energy Vanguard Blog*, July 6, 2011. http://www.energyvanguard.com/blog-building-science-HERS-BPI/bid/40016/The-Magic-of-Cold-Part-1-How-Your-Air-Conditioner-Works

69 "5 Habits for Maintaining a Clean and Organized Home," How Jen Does It Youtube Channel, June 6, 2016. https://www.youtube.com/watch?v=CXRiDkKNEPE

70 Becky, "The Organically Clean Home," *Clean Mama*, February 23, 2014. http://www.cleanmama.net/2014/02/guess-what-2.html

71 "How Not to use your Air Conditioning," *Mr. Money Mustache*, July 18, 2011. http://www.mrmoneymustache.com/2011/07/18/how-not-to-use-your-air-conditioning/

72 "Acclimatization: Adjusting to the Temperature," University of Iowa Hospitals & Clinics, accessed June 2016. https://www.uihealthcare.org/health-library/acclimatization-adjusting-to-the-temperature/

73 Tris Thorp, "Transition to Fall: How to Stay Healthy Through the Season Change," The Chopra Center, accessed June 2016. http://www.chopra.com/ccl/transition-to-fall-how-to-stay-health-through-the-season-change

74 Blair Badenhop, "4 Ways to Support Your Body During Seasonal Transitions," *Parsley Blog*, October 1, 2015. https://parsleyhealth.com/seasonal-transitions/

75 Martin Holladay, "Bathroom Exhaust Fans," *Musings of an Energy Nerd*, August 7, 2014.

http://www.greenbuildingadvisor.com/blogs/dept/musings/bathroom-exhaust-fans

76"From Clammy To Comfortable: Tackling Bathroom Humidity," Mitsubishi Electric, accessed June 2016. http://www.mitsubishicomfort.com/articles/air-quality/indoor-air-quality/from-clammy-to-comfortable-tackling-bathroom-humidity

77"The 7 Best Energy Efficiency Apps for Your Smartphone and a Greener Lifestyle," *Service Champions Blog*, October 19, 2015. http://www.servicechampions.net/blog/the-7-best-energy-efficiency-apps-for-your-smartphone-and-a-greener-lifestyle/

78 "WattzOn." WattzOn, accessed June 2016. http://www.wattzon.com/

79"Find a Program," Energy Star, accessed June 2016. https://www.energystar.gov/index.cfm?fuseaction=hpwes_profiles.showFindaProgram

80"Spring Home Maintenance," Martha Stewart Living Omnipedia, Inc. published 2009, accessed June 2016. http://images.marthastewart.com/images/content/web/pdfs/checklists/ms_checklist_springhome.pdf

81Danny Lipford, "Using Shade to Reduce Energy Bills," *Today's Homeowner*, accessed June 2016. http://www.todayshomeowner.com/video/using-shade-to-reduce-energy-bills/

82Don Vandervort, "How to Weatherstrip a Door," HomeTips.com, April 20, 2016. http://www.hometips.com/diy-how-to/weatherstripping-doors.html

83 Rachel Cluett, "Small actions that add up to large energy savings for Earth Day," *ACEEE Blog,* April 22, 2014. http://aceee.org/blog/2014/04/small-actions-add-large-energy-saving

84"Weatherstripping," Energy.Gov, accessed June 2016. http://energy.gov/energysaver/weatherstripping

85Mihai-Emilian Blaga, "13 Ways to Save Power By Tweaking Power Plans in Windows," *Digital Citizen*, September 10, 2015. http://www.digitalcitizen.life/how-tweak-advanced-settings-power-plan-windows-7?page=1

86John Schueler, "Are Energy Vampires Sucking You Dry?" Energy.Gov, October 29, 2015. http://energy.gov/articles/are-energy-vampires-sucking-you-dry

87"How to Save Energy by eliminating Phantom Loads," *eartheasy,* February 9, 2010. http://learn.eartheasy.com/2010/02/5-ways-to-save-energy-by-eliminating-phantom-loads/

88Barry Fischer and Nate Kaufman, "America's most unpopular way of saving energy…is one of Europe's favorites," *Opower*

Blog, July 31, 2013. https://blog.opower.com/2013/07/americas-most-unpopular-way-of-saving-energy-is-one-of-europes-favorites/

89Erin Raub, "Benefits of Motion Sensors and Detectors," *SafeSoundFamily,* updated February 18, 2016. http://safesoundfamily.com/blog/benefits-of-motion-sensors-and-detectors/

90Brittany Bailey, "How to Install an Exterior Motion Sensor Light," *Pretty Handy Girl*, November 17, 2014. http://www.prettyhandygirl.com/install-exterior-motion-sensor-light/

91Martin Holladay, "Is Your Pool an Energy Hog?" *Musings of an Energy Nerd*, May 31, 2013. http://www.greenbuildingadvisor.com/blogs/dept/musings/your-pool-energy-hog

92Martin Holladay, "Can Swimming Pools Be Green?" *Musings of an Energy Nerd,* May 12, 2009. http://www.greenbuildingadvisor.com/blogs/dept/musings/can-swimming-pools-be-green

93"Pool Pump Efficiency," Saturn Resource Management, accessed June 2016. http://blog.srmi.biz/energy-saving-tips/appliances-energy-efficiency/pool-pump-efficiency/

94Barry Fischer, "Homes with pools use 49% more electricity per year, but it's not just because of the pool," *Opower Blog,* July 26, 2012. https://blog.opower.com/2012/07/homes-with-pools-use-

49-more-electricity-but-its-not-just-because-of-the-pool/

95"Solar Swimming Pool Heaters," Energy.Gov, accessed June 2016. http://energy.gov/energysaver/solar-swimming-pool-heaters

96Scott Cooney, "Refrigerator and freezer temperatures and humidities for efficient operation," *Green Living Ideas*, accessed June 2016. http://greenlivingideas.com/2013/05/15/refrigerator-freezer-ideal-temperatures-humidities-forefficient-operation/

97"Kitchen Appliances," Energy.Gov, accessed June 2016. http://energy.gov/energysaver/kitchen-appliances

98"Lower Bills With Low-Flow Faucets," HGTV, accessed June 2016. http://www.hgtv.com/remodel/interior-remodel/lower-bills-with-low-flow-faucets

99 "What is WaterSense?" EPA, accessed June 2016. https://www3.epa.gov/watersense/about_us/what_is_ws.html

100Pablo Paster, "Ask Pablo: Is It Really Worth Insulating My Pipes?" Treehugger, January 16, 2012. http://www.treehugger.com/energy-efficiency/ask-pablo-it-really-worth-insulating-my-pipes.html

101"Tips: Water Heating," Energy.Gov, accessed June 2016. http://energy.gov/energysaver/tips-water-heating

102Karen Wirth, "Plug That Water Leak And Drop The Waste: Fix A Leak Week," *Sustainablog*, accessed June 2016. http://sustainablog.org/2015/03/plug-that-water-leak-and-drop-the-waste-fix-a-leak-week/

103"TZOA Wearable Enviro-Tracker," TZOA, accessed June 2016. http://www.tzoa.com/#homepage

104"Home-Nest" Nest Labs, accessed June 2016. https://nest.com/

105Matt Goering, "The Benefits of Weather Stripping," HomeAdvisor, accessed June 2016. http://www.homeadvisor.com/article.show.The-Benefits-of-Weather-Stripping.9382.html

106"Weatherstripping," Energy.Gov, accessed June 2016. http://energy.gov/energysaver/weatherstripping

107US DOE, *Weatherize Your Home—Caulk and Weather Strip* (Washington, DC: NREL, 2001). http://www.nrel.gov/docs/fy01osti/28039.pdf

108Allan Chen, "Why Fluorescent Lighting Isn't Dead," Lawrence Berkeley National Laboratory, Spring 2011. http://eetd.lbl.gov/newsletter/nl35/eetd-nl35-6-fluorescent.html

109Karen Tetlow, "Task Lighting Solutions: Their Economic and Ergonomic Benefits," McGraw Hill Construction, November

2007. http://construction.com/ce/articles/0711humanscale-6.asp

110Contech Lighting, *Residential Lighting Guide* (Illinois: Conservation Technology of Illinois, LLC, 2014). http://www.contechlighting.com/sites/default/files/contechresiden taillightingguide.pdf

111Mark Hogrebe, "Putting Light Where It's Needed: The Benefits of Task Lighting," Dazor Lighting Solutions, accessed June 2016. https://www.dazor.com/task-lighting-benefits.html

112"Top 10 Energy Benefits of Light Control," Lutron, accessed June 2016. http://www.lutron.com/en-US/Education-Training/Pages/LCE/GreenBenefits.aspx

113Jane Lockhart, "Wall colours, lighting & efficiency: Advice from a designer," BC Hydro, January 31, 2012. https://www.bchydro.com/news/conservation/2012/wall_colours_and_lighting.html

114Science Buddies, "Simmering Science: Can Your House's Color Reduce Your Summer Energy Bill?" *Scientific American*, July 26, 2012. http://www.scientificamerican.com/article/bring-science-home-house-color-heat/

115"Color & Energy Matters," Color Matters, accessed June 2016. http://www.colormatters.com/color-and-science/color-and-energy-matters

116"Refrigerators and Freezers," Consumer Energy Center, accessed June 2016. http://www.consumerenergycenter.org/residential/appliances/refrigerators.html

117"Made of Progress," Levi's, accessed June 2016. http://www.levi.com/US/en_US/madeofprogress#

118"Water<Less," Levi Strauss & Co., accessed June 2016. http://www.levistrauss.com/sustainability/products/waterless/

119"Tips & Tricks for Conserving Energy," *The Laundress blog,* July 6, 2012. http://blog.thelaundress.com/wordpress/project/tips-tricks-for-conserving-energy/

120"Clothes Dryer Fires in Residential Buildings," *Topical Fire Report Series* 13.7 (August 2012) 1-6. https://www.usfa.fema.gov/downloads/pdf/statistics/v13i7.pdf

121"Consumer Product Safety Commission," CPSC, accessed June 2016. http://www.cpsc.gov/

122"Buying a New Dryer," Smarter House, accessed June 2016. http://smarterhouse.org/laundry/buying-new-dryer

123Jason Fitzpatrick, "Batch Oven Use for a Cooler Summer Kitchen," *Lifehacker*, July 7, 2010. http://lifehacker.com/5581379/batch-oven-use-for-a-cooler-summer-kitchen

124Emma Christensen, "Stay Cool! Make Your Oven Work Double Time," *kitchn*, July 6, 2010. http://www.thekitchn.com/stay-cool-make-your-oven-work-120477

125"Stoves, Ranges and Ovens," Consumer Energy Center, accessed June 2016. http://www.consumerenergycenter.org/residential/appliances/ranges.html

126Ben Morelli, "How cooking method and practice affects energy consumption," Yale Environment Review, January 14, 2014. http://environment.yale.edu/yer/article/how-cooking-method-and-practice-affects-energy-consumption#gsc.tab=0

127"Energy Star @ home tips," Energy Star, accessed June 2016. https://www.energystar.gov/products/energy_star_home_tips

128Rachel Sanders, "27 Clever New Ways to Use Kitchen Appliances," *BuzzFeed*, December 31, 2013. https://www.buzzfeed.com/rachelysanders/clever-new-ways-to-use-kitchen-appliances?utm_term=.kdLvz94XR6#.xpjgB5zoAW

129Sherry Gray, "Are Crock Pots Economical?" UCONN College of Agriculture, Health, & Natural Resources, accessed 2016. http://sustainableliving.uconn.edu/articles/crockpots.php

130"Consortium for Energy Efficiency," CEE, accessed June

2016. http://www.cee1.org/

131"Dishwashers," Consumer Energy Center, accessed June 2016. http://www.consumerenergycenter.org/residential/appliances/dishwashers.html

132"Do Eco Settings on Your Appliances Really Save Energy?" Mister Sparky, February 17, 2016. http://www.mistersparky.com/Blog/do-eco-settings-on-your-appliances-really-save-energy

133Harold McGee, "A Hot-Water Bath for Thawing Meats," *New York Times*, June 6, 2011. http://www.nytimes.com/2011/06/08/dining/a-hot-water-bath-for-thawing-meats-the-curious-cook.html?_r=1

134Martin Holladay, "Makeup Air for Range Hoods," *Musings of an Energy Nerd*, November19, 2010. http://www.greenbuildingadvisor.com/blogs/dept/musings/makeup-air-range-hoods

135"ASHRAE," Wikipedia, accessed June 2016. https://en.wikipedia.org/wiki/ASHRAE

136Matt Hickman, "Weatherize this: Chimney Balloons," *mother nature network,* December 21, 2009. http://www.mnn.com/your-home/at-home/blogs/weatherize-this-chimney-balloons

137Ask Umbra, "Baths vs. showers, an eco-smackdown," Grist,

February 26, 2015. http://grist.org/living/baths-vs-showers-an-eco-smackdown/

138"Guide to Greywater-Compatible Cleaning Products," Ecology Center, accessed June 2016. http://ecologycenter.org/factsheets/greywater-cleaning-products/

139"Skin Deep Cosmetics," EWG, accessed June 2016. http://www.ewg.org/skindeep/

140Barry Fischer, "Hot and heavy energy usage: How the demand and price for electricity skyrocketed on a 100° day," *Opower Blog*, September 5, 2012. https://blog.opower.com/2012/09/hot-and-heavy-energy-usage-how-the-demand-and-price-for-electricity-skyrocketed-on-a-100-day/

141"Why Buy Local?" Sustainable Connections, accessed June 2016. http://sustainableconnections.org/thinklocal/why

142Rachel Koning Beals, "How Consumers and Communities Can Benefit From 'Buying Local,'" *U.S. News*, October 28, 2011. http://money.usnews.com/money/personal-finance/articles/2011/10/28/how-consumers-and-communities-can-benefit-from-buying-local

143John Tierney, "How Virtuous is Ed Begley Jr.?" *New York Times*, February 25, 2008.

http://tierneylab.blogs.nytimes.com/2008/02/25/how-virtuous-is-ed-begley-jr/

144Michael Cohen and Matthew Heberger, "Driving vs. Walking: Cows, Climate Change, and Choice" (Oakland: Pacific Institute, 2008). http://www.pacinst.org/app/uploads/2013/02/driving_vs_walking 3.pdf

145"It's Easy Being Green: Walking vs. Driving Is a No-Brainer," *American Progress*, July 2, 2008. https://www.americanprogress.org/issues/green/news/2008/07/02/4723/its-easy-being-green-walking-vs-driving-is-a-no-brainer/

146American Public Transit Association, "Public Transportation Saves Energy and Helps Our Environment," APTA, accessed June 2016. http://www.apta.com/gap/policyresearch/Documents/facts_environment_09.pdf

147"Attention drivers! Turn off your idling engines," EDF, accessed June 2016. https://www.edf.org/climate/reports/idling

148Allison Bailes "Case Closed: Get Those Air Conditioning Ducts out of the Attic" Energy Vanguard accessed June 2016 http://www.energyvanguard.com/blog-building-science-HERS-BPI/bid/38931/Case-Closed-Get-Those-Air-Conditioning-Ducts-out-of-the-Attic

149"Top Ten Things About Air Conditioning" ASHRAE, accessed June 2016 https://www.ashrae.org/resources--

publications/free-resources/top-ten-things-about-air-conditioning

150"Maintaining Your Air Conditioner" U.S. Department of Energy, accessed June 2016
http://energy.gov/energysaver/maintaining-your-air-conditioner

151Parker, D., Barkaszi, S., Sonne. J., "Measured Impacts of Air Conditioner Condenser Shading" Presented at The Tenth Symposium on Improving Building Systems in Hot and Humid Climates, Texas A & M University, Fort Worth, TX, May 13-14 1996, accessed June 2016
http://www.fsec.ucf.edu/en/publications/html/FSEC-PF-302-96/

152"Elements of An Energy Efficient House" National Renewable Energy Laboratory, July 2000
http://www.nrel.gov/docs/fy00osti/27835.pdf

153John Krigger, *Residential Energy: Cost Savings and Comfort for Existing Buildings (6th Edition)* (New York: Pearson, 2013).

154John Krigger, *Residential Energy: Cost Savings and Comfort for Existing Buildings (6th Edition)* (New York: Pearson, 2013).

155Joseph Lstiburek, "BSD-012 Moisture Control for New Residential Buildings" Building Science Corporation March 9th 2009, accessed June 2016
http://buildingscience.com/documents/digests/bsd-012-moisture-control-for-new-residential-buildings

156"Energy Efficiency Improvements Have Largely Offset Effect of More, Larger Homes" U.S. Energy Information Administration, February 18th 2015 accessed June 2016 http://www.eia.gov/todayinenergy/detail.cfm?id=20031

www.ingramcontent.com/pod-product-compliance
Lightning Source LLC
Chambersburg PA
CBHW051426090426
42737CB00014B/2845